MEGALITHIC M
OF CORN\

Cheryl Straffon

MEYN MAMVRO PUBLICATIONS

i

MEGALITHIC MYSTERIES OF CORNWALL

First published in 2004 by Meyn Mamvro Publications, 51 Carn Bosavern, St.Just, Penzance, Cornwall TR19 7QX

Web site: www.meynmamvro.co.uk

ISBN: 0 9518859 8 7

An investigation into the strange and anomalous energies at ancient sites in Cornwall, based on research and ideas from the fields of earth mysteries, archaeology, legend and folklore. The book includes topics such as Ley Lines, Energy Lines, Radiation, Magnetism, Ultrasound, Strange Lights, Alignments, Ghost Roads, Mythic Pathways, Piskey Paths, and Altered States of Consciousness. This is the first time all this material has been brought together in one book, and it adds a new dimension to any visit to sacred sites in the mysterious land of Cornwall.

Cheryl Straffon is the author of the acclaimed books on Cornwall: *"Pagan Cornwall: Land of the Goddess", "Fentynyow Kernow – In search of Cornwall's holy wells",* and *"The Earth Mysteries Guides to Ancient Sites in Cornwall".* She lives and works in West Cornwall, where her knowledge and love of the sites and their mysteries is well-known and much respected.

CONTENTS

iii

INTRODUCTION

This book came about after I had finished researching and writing the *Earth Mysteries Guides to Ancient Sites in Cornwall* (3 volumes) and *Pagan Cornwall – Land of the Goddess*. The former Guides aimed to give a concise yet comprehensive insight into the locations of ancient and sacred sites in Cornwall, together with some details of the possible meaning and significance of these very special places. *Pagan Cornwall,* on the other hand, provided the matrix for the *Guides:* a history of Cornwall from a pagan perspective, that used the elements of archaeology, prehistory, legend and folklore to tease out a continuity of understanding of the people who built the sites, and to give some possible insights into their beliefs and ideas. It traced the belief of Goddess throughout the millennia, from the early megalithic builders through the Celtic era , and brought the story up to the present day, and the revival of Goddess and pagan celebration in Cornwall today.

However, when these books were finished, I became aware that there was much still unsaid about the sites, and the discoveries that have been made at these places over the last couple of decades or so. In particular, the work of the Dragon Project in the late 1980s, and the formation of the Cornish Earth Mysteries Group in 1990 gave a new impetus to the study of the sites. As one of the founder members of the CEMG, and still being on the Committee, those last 14 years have given me much valuable shared information, ideas and perspectives on the sites in Cornwall. In that time there have been nearly 100 talks (not all on Cornwall of course), and nearly 70 walks and site visits throughout Cornwall. There has been a large volume of material that has accumulated during all those talks and visits, some of it anecdotal, some of it scientific, or quasi-scientific, some of it much more intuitive and personal. Some of this material has been published in the on-going magazine that I edit *Meyn Mamvro (Ancient Stones and Sacred Sites in Cornwall),* that has now been going 18 years, and has produced well over 50 issues on all aspects of Cornish material, including Earth Energies, Ancient Stones, Sacred Sites, Paganism, Leypaths, Cornish Pre-History and Culture, Megalithic Mysteries, and Legends and Folklore. Much of this material is scattered throughout the magazines, and in this current book has been brought together in a coherent framework for the first time.

In addition, over the years I have been privileged to have been the recipient of many stories and experiences that various people have told me about the sites and what happened to them there. Some of these stories are personal to the people who would not wish them to be published; others, however, are willing to share these experiences with others, in the wish that they may be recorded for posterity, and perhaps in the hope that there may be some feedback from others who have experienced similar events. Some of these experiences have also found their way into this book. Most of these people are named, or given initials, and my thanks goes to them for allowing their experiences to be recorded, for many of them are truly fascinating and very curious. Finally, I have also had a close look at the books of folklore and stories collected respectively by Robert Hunt and William Bottrell in the late 19th century, to see what these tales can tell us about the experiences and beliefs of the Cornish people from only just over a century ago. This mixture of research, personal experience and folklore and legend has been woven together to see if it can give us a deeper insight into the nature and purpose of the ancient and sacred sites in Cornwall today.

The book starts with a look at ley lines, and tries to sort out what different people mean by this term. There would be enough material here for a book in itself, so this is of necessity only a brief glimpse. From here, we move naturally into so-called 'Energy Lines', and try and place the subject into some kind of meaningful framework. Then the next few chapters look at the work of the Dragon Project and the CEMG at the ancient sites, and what has been discovered about radiation anomalies, magnetism and electro-magnetic effects, anomalous sounds and strange lights. There is now quite a considerable body of research that has built up over the last 20 years, much of it not widely known about, even in Cornwall. From strange lights we move to look at how the ancient sites were deliberately aligned to the sun, moon and stars: much of this material was pioneered by the Earth Mysteries researchers from the 1970s onwards, and dismissed by archaeologists as the "lunatic fringe". Of course, needless to say, the new generation of archaeologists are now discovering this material for themselves, even if they do not always acknowledge their debt to the early pioneers! Finally, the last 4 chapters of the book move into the area of altered states of consciousness, and the Other world of spirits, ghosts, fairies and paranormal experiences.

My thanks go to all the people, some named, but many not, who contributed their research, ideas, insights and experiences that have gone to weave a fascinating tapestry of a picture of "strangeness" at the ancient sites. I believe that this is the first book on Cornwall to bring all this material together and link it up in a coherent way. I hope you will be inspired, intrigued and excited by some at least of the content of this book, and that it will encourage you to go and have a look at some of these sites yourself, and see what you think and feel and experience there.

Chapter 1 Following the Ley of the Land
Ley Lines and aligned sites

We start our quest into Cornwall's strange phenomena with a look at Leys, or, as they are often called, Ley Lines. Of course, everyone knows what Leys are, don't they? Well, actually, people are often talking about different things, or a combination of things, when they talk about Leys. We could start by trying to disentangle some of the meanings attributed to the word.

- An alignment of sites that stretches across the land in a straight line (once described by John Michell as 'rifle-barrel accuracy'). These sites usually include one or more megalithic monuments (sometimes from different periods of time), but may also include more recent features, such as Churches, and even natural features, such as Scotch Pine trees. The term 'Ley' to describe such a line of sites was first coined by Alfred Watkins in the 1920s, and he came to believe that they were the remnants of ancient trackways. In Cornwall, the study of such alignments was given a boost by John Michell who researched nearly 50 of them and published the results in *The Old Stones of Land's End*[1].

- An invisible line of "energy" that runs across the earth and through ancient and modern sites. This line of energy can be dowsed by means of dowsing rods or other implements. Many of these lines have been identified, and there are usually several at most of Cornwall's well-known sites. The most-well known exponents of these lines and the dowsing of them are Hamish Miller, who, together with the late Don Wilkins, brought the subject into public consciousness. A good summary of such energy dowsing can be found in Hamish Miller's book *It's Not Too Late*[2]

- A wide line that runs across long distances, linking together sacred sites. This line is more-or-less straight, though it may be curvilinear in places. This line can also be dowsed, and is generally thought to have spiritual or mystical significance. It has sometimes been criticised as actually not being precise enough over long distances due to the curvature of the earth, and a

---

[1] John Michell *The Old Stones of Land's End* [Garnstone Press, 1974]
[2] Hamish Miller *It's Not Too Late* [Penwith Press,1998]

more accurate term might be 'geomantic corridor'. The most famous example is the Michael line (so named after many hilltop sites on its alignment which have churches dedicated to St.Michael), running through Cornwall and up to the east of England. This was first identified by John Michell in the 1960s and given a revival in the 1990s in the immensely popular book by Hamish Miller and Paul Broadhurst *The Sun and the Serpent*[3]. In this book the authors also identified another such 'mega-line' that they called the Mary Line, that was more serpentine and linked up sites such as wells, springs, etc. Subsequently, Broadhurst found two other such lines, that he called the Merlin and Morgana lines[4], and, more recently, Broadhurst and Miller have tracked two international lines they named the Apollo and Athena lines from Skellig Michael off Ireland, through west Cornwall and St.Michael's Mount, across Europe to Armageddon in Israel.[5]

In addition to these 'ley' lines, there are also alignments of two or more ancient sites in close proximity (such as stone circle and outlying standing stone) that line up with significant natural landscape features, such as hills or tors, and/or with significant astronomical events, such as sun and moon rises and settings. These we shall explore in Ch.7 (Astronomical Alignments). Finally, there are direct lines running across shortish stretches of land that seem to have been used in medieval times for the transportation of coffins, some of which have legends of ghosts or myths associated with them, which we shall explore in Ch.8 (Ghost Roads & Mythic Pathways).

But, let us begin with the 'classic' Leys, first given prominence in Cornwall by John Michell in *The Old Stones of Land's End.* To give a flavour of these, I have selected one of the most impressive, that runs for about 6½ miles across the northern moors of West Penwith.

---

[3] Hamish Miller & Paul Broadhurst *The Sun and the Serpent* [Pendragon Press, 1989]
[4] Paul Broadhurst *Tintagel and the Arthurian Mythos* [Pendragon Press, 1992]
[5] Paul Broadhust & Hamish Miller *The Dance of the Dragon* [Pendragon Press, 2000]

The Ley begins on the very edge of the northern coastline, just outside of St.Just at **Carn Gluze/Ballowal Barrow** [SW3555 3124]. This is a Neolithic chambered tomb lying within a large barrow, some 40ft across. Although it has been much disturbed by Borlase's excavations in 1878, nevertheless the entrance grave and two internal cists can be seen, as well as the thick walls of the barrow.

↓

From here, looking one way the western ocean can be seen, and looking the other, along the direction of the Ley, Tregeseal Common about 2 miles away. On the edge of the Common in a field at SW3805 3212 is **Tregeseal Chambered Cairn** with an oval mound and two roofing slabs covering a chamber 11ft long and 4ft wide. The Ley passes the edge of this cairn, and links together these two powerful burial sites.

↓

A short distance of about ½ mile along the direction of the Ley leads to **Tregeseal Stone Circle** [SW3866 3238] more properly called Tregeseal East, as there was formerly another circle to the west, and perhaps a third as well. This is a 'classic' West Penwith stone circle with 19 stones, of which more will be said in future chapters. The Ley passes right through the centre of this circle.

↓

From this circle, the Ley continues to run in a straight line to **Boswens menhir** [SW4001 3290], the tip of which is just visible from the circle. Sir Norman Lockyer first noticed this alignment in 1909, and said that it marked the May Day sunrise, though when the CEMG went to observe it in 1991, the sun rose 1° south of the actual menhir. Nevertheless, it is still an impressive alignment.

From Boswens, the Ley continues in a north-east direction to **West Lanyon Quoit** [SW4231 3379], a ruined megalithic structure that would originally have been of the same kind as nearby Lanyon & Chûn Quoits. Boswens menhir is not quite visible from the site, but if it was originally covered with a mound, as some archaeologists believe, then the menhir would have been visible from the top.

↓

Finally, the Ley ends at **Mulfra Courtyard House Settlement** [SW4539 3496], which consists of at least four courtyardhouses together with other hut circles. This site is larger than the other individual sites, and also dates from a later period (Iron Age). Nevertheless 6 sites, 5 of which are near-contemporary, aligned over a distance of 6½ miles is an impressive record.

In addition, some years ago John Michell and myself went to have a look for possible lost stones between some of the points on the Ley and found a significant stone in a hedge at SW4270 3395 in a field further on from West Lanyon Quoit, and visible from the Quoit. It may well be that there are many other such stones to be found marking intermediary points along many of the leys, making each point intervisible with the next. This could be an interesting project for anyone with the time and enthusiasm to follow it up.

This is just one Ley out of about 50 identified by Michell in his book and in later revisions. In addition, other Leys have been identified by other researchers in the pages of *Meyn Mamvro* magazine over the last 18 years, so that the total for West Penwith in Cornwall is now about 70. These have been all collated and listed by researcher Raymond Cox, and are available on floppy disk or print-out from the *Meyn Mamvro* address. In his introduction to his paper Cox says:

"At least 70 alignments have been found, many by John Michell, which he reported in his book *"The Old Stones of Land's End"*; some by *"Meyn Mamvro"* magazine; and a few extra by myself. Many link ancient sites and some with both prehistoric and more modern sites. There are bound to be links in such a small area. However, the smaller the area the more exact can be the lines - it seems to apply here. Michell's leys were found to be mostly very accurate, average width being 1 metre, and a maximum of 7 metres.
Sites include tumuli, menhirs, stone circles, Iron Age courtyard house settlements, (though these cover large areas), hillforts, wayside crosses of the Dark Ages and early Christian era, holy wells, parish churches and even stretches of parish boundaries (at least 4 lines). Also in some places lengths of ancient tracks are part of the ley. The lines range from a maximum of 8 sites in alignment down to 3. There could be others on some of the alignments which could perhaps be found by walking the lines where this is possible. But there is also the question of missing and destroyed sites. Some alignments discussed in *"Meyn Mamvro"* magazine were found as a result of the discovery - or identification - in recent years, of 2 menhirs, those of Newham Farm and Ennis Farm, in hedges."

Raymond Cox goes on to say that some of the megalithic sites appear to be 'nodal' sites, that is, they have a larger-than-average set of lines going through them. The most significant of these is Carfury Menhir [SW4400 3400], a hidden standing stone in a lovely setting near to Bosiliack, surrounded by bluebells in the spring. This stone has no less than 8 lines of alignments passing through it, which makes it a real 'hot spot' for alignments in West Penwith. The full list of nodal sites is as follows:-

1 Carfury menhir –[SW4400 3400] - 8 lines
2 Tresvennack Pillar menhir [SW4418 2788] - 5 lines
3 Drift menhirs, a pair [SW4371 2831] - 4 lines
4 The Pipers menhirs [SW4353 2482 & 4350 2474] - 5 lines
5 Destroyed (missing) menhir at Brea [SW3814 2799] - 5 lines
6 Menhir at Redhouse –[SW4480 2663] - 5 lines
7 Trelew menhir [SW4217 2693] - 4 lines
8 Boscawen-ûn stone circle [SW4122 2736] - 7 lines.
9 Tregeseal stone circle [SW3866 3238] - 4 lines
10 Tregiffian Vean chambered tomb [SW3725 2774] - 4 lines
11. Bosiliack barrow [SW4311 3422]- 4 lines
12. West Lanyon quoit – [SW4231 3379] - 4 lines
13. King Arthur's Stone, Sennen [SW3599 2540] – 5 lines

Of course, not everyone accepts the existence or veracity of these Leys, especially archaeologists, who are wont to put it all down to chance or coincidence. However, some statistical analysis has been done on the West Cornwall sites, and shown to be greater than average statistical probability. In addition, there are several examples of alignment of sites over much shorter distances. The stone row at Zennor [SW4539 3881] would be one example; another is the line of (mainly holed) stones near the Merry Maidens, running from the (site of) a holed stone in hedge [SW4227 2421], through Tregiffian Barrow [SW4303 2442], the remains of a holed stone on the ground at SW4315 2450, a holed stone used as a gatepost [SW4324 2457], the Nun Careg cross [SW4329 2460] to a holed stone in the wall of a mowhay at SW4365 2489. This is a line of 6 sites over a distance of only 1300 yards, a pretty impressive alignment. So, even if we do not accept each and every Ley proposed as equally significant, we can at least see that there is something going on here that lies beyond the limits of probability. The next question then, is of course, why?

Why should ancient peoples want or need to place their sites in alignment with each other over longish distances across the land? That they were capable of doing so is not beyond doubt – even archaeologists accept that stone rows, reaves, boundary walls, and so on were laid out in straight lines, so it is perfectly feasible for other sites to be set up in the same way. There is no one clear answer to this conundrum, but some of the possibilities are looked at in the following pages. These include astronomical significances, lines marking spirit paths across the land, invisible to ordinary vision (like the Aboriginal 'song lines'), and perhaps 'energy lines' that ancient peoples could sense and tap in to. And it is to these energy lines that we now turn our attention.

Chapter 2   The Power of the Earth's Energy
Energy Lines and dowsing

People talk rather glibly about "energy lines", but what is meant exactly by the term? There are many different kinds of "energy" on the Earth: electromagnetic energy, radio waves from outer space, natural radiation from the rocks and stones, etc. Many dowsers say that they can distinguish different kinds of energy, each of which has a different frequency or 'signature', and they have different systems to distinguish them, sometimes involving different colours or different names. Other dowsers seem to be able to 'tune in' to underground streams and 'blind springs', many of which are often found to lie beneath ancient sites, such as stone circles. Very often, dowsers do identify the same 'energy lines' at a site, but in many cases different dowsers find different lines and patterns, and sometimes these are contradictory in nature. So, despite what some dowsers might like to claim, tapping into energy lines is not an exact science, and is often a very personal and individual response to what is there.

It does become more interesting, and sometimes more verifiable, when a group of dowsers come together at a site to see what they can collectively find. Over the last 15 years or so, the Cornish Earth Mysteries Group has visited different sites, and dowsing there has often produced some fascinating results. At a Dowsing Day at Chûn Quoit [SW4023 3396] in April 1990 with Don Wilkins, an energy line was found by several people, running from Chûn Castle [SW4050 3400] through Chûn Quoit and on to the distinctive rocky outcrop of Carn Kenidjack. This line also 'coincidentally' marks the midwinter solstice sunset alignment in a notch on the Carn [see Ch.7]. A spiral energy pattern was also dowsed inside the Quoit itself. This is a similar pattern to that found at other sites, such as at the Merry Maidens near Lamorna [SW4327 2451], where Hamish Miller found spiral energy patterns coming from each of the stones and lines of energy flowing out from the site.[6] In April 1991 the Group went to Tregeseal Circle [SW3866 3238] where they found six underground streams weaving through the circle and meeting at a point slightly off the geometric centre (where a low magnotometer reading was also obtained). The Group also dowsed for the position of the now-destroyed western circle, and found

---

[6] Hamish Miller *It's Not Too Late* [Penwith Press, 1998] p.99.

positions of 19 original stones, though interestingly not in exactly the same place as indicated on an early map.

Dowsing at Chûn Quoit – April 1990

A visit to the Nine Maidens Stone Circle at Boskednan [SW4343 3512] also revealed six curving underground water lines, meeting at a point just offset from the geometrical centre of the circle, the same as at Tregeseal, and surely not a coincidence. One dowser found 49 radial energy lines coming from the energy centre of the circle, but other variable numbers were found, showing how difficult it is to be sure of what is being found, and the advisability of finding some way to corroborate results.

In August 1991 the Group visited the Merry Maidens stone circle [SW4327 2451] mentioned above, and found the same energy lines as those identified by Hamish Miller, and there was also a great measure of agreement between the dowsers as to what lines there were and the direction they flowed. The productive uses to which dowsing can be put was also demonstrated by one dowser who followed the direction of a previously-identified Ley Line running north-westwards from the circle and discovered a significant stone in a hedge on the line at SW4322 2483. It does appear that Ley Lines can be dowsed energetically, as well as being followed on maps and across the land. But while Ley Lines may also be energy lines (or at least are able to be dowsed), not all energy lines are Ley Lines, that is, they run across the land but do not necessarily link together ancient sites. While at the Merry Maidens, nearby Tregiffian Barrow [SW4303 2442] was dowsed, and a spiral energy pattern, similar to that found inside Chûn Quoit was found by several people.

Boscawen-ûn stone circle [SW4122 2736] has also been dowsed, particularly thoroughly by Hamish Miller, who found a strong energy line (the "Mary line") entering the circle at an angle 13° east of north, but then turning at the base of the centre standing stone and veering off at an angle of 53° east of north that corresponded with ridge of the leaning monument. Another strong energy line from the south-west was found going over the quartz stone and then stopping at the centre stone, with other lines leaving to the north and east. Hamish Miller comments: "The impression was of a nerve ganglion, a crucial point of exchange and interaction in a nervous system that was alive and functioning irrespective of whether Homo Sapiens comprehended it or not".[7] Hamish has also found spiral energy patterns at the nearby Blind Fiddler standing stone [SW4252 2818], similar to the Merry Maidens stones, and those found by the CEMG at Chûn Quoit and Tregiffian Barrow. But according to Hamish, at this standing stone, the energy spirals around the stone clockwise at the waxing moon and then reverses polarity at the waning moon.

A particularly interesting dowsing day took place at the Nine Maidens stone row on St.Breock Downs [SW9363 6745] in August 1995. As well as the stone row, another site called 'The Nine Sisters', which may have been a circle or a double stone row, was mentioned and illustrated by John Norden in 1728[8] No-one knows exactly where this site was, or indeed what it was, but on this day the team of 6 dowsers found some remarkable results. Sometimes working 'blind', to reduce the possibility of being influenced by each other, the team walked the length of the field and found that there were formerly 13 stones in the now 9-stone row, with a stone setting at the north end. Continuing southwards, they found another 25 points, and subsequent searching of the ditch revealed one of the stones (a 6ft 4in shaped stone) lying there. A second stone row with the same number of stones was found approximately 25ft to the west of the first . Could this have been the missing Nine Sisters row? We cannot be sure, but it shows that dowsing throws up some very interesting possibilities.

---

[7] Hamish Miller *Dowsing at Boscawen-ûn Circle* [Meyn Mamvro, no.12 p.8-9]
[8] John Norden *Topographical and Historical Description of Cornwall* [c1603-7, printed 1728, re-issued 1966] p.48

Dowsing at the Nine Maidens row – Aug 1995

The ability of dowsers to find lost or destroyed sites is one of the most valuable aspects of the skill. Locating the second circle at Tregeseal [SW3861 3237] has already been mentioned, and the same dowsing activity took place during a CEMG visit to the Nine Maidens, Wendron [SW6829 3656], where the Group also located the missing stones in the second circle. An unusual use of dowsing skills occurred at the site of the Devil's Quoit [SW9232 6193] near St.Columb Major. The monument was broken up and lost by the end of the 19th Century, but in 1977 the Cornwall Committee for Rescue Archaeology and St. Columb Old Cornwall Society (hardly radical alternative groups!) dowsed the site and found the location of the buried capstone! When the spot was dug up, the capstone was indeed found, and now stands beside a minor road off the A39.

Showing that dowsers can find the location of lost and missing stones is some way from the discussion of energy lines, but of course they are all interrelated, as it is often during the process of following the energy line that missing stones come to light. Sometimes, these energy lines do not follow expected or obvious paths. For example, when CEMG dowsed the Wendron Nine Maidens circles in June 2002, a very powerful energy line was found running to the nearby Hangman's Barrow [SW6737 3669], but it came not from the existing SE circle [SW6831 3653], but from the site of the destroyed NW one [SW6829 3656]. And sometimes it is not just the ancient sites that have powerful energy lines, but also natural features. Again, on the CEMG June 2002 visit, it was a natural logan (rocking) stone at Mên Amber [SW6501 3225] that seemed to have a very powerful energy source. Of course, we should not be surprised at this: ancient peoples were not only connected to the megalithic monuments they had built, but also the natural features of the Land that were significant to them, such as Tors, Carns and unusual rocks.

So, what exactly are these "energy lines"? We can dowse them, some people can even feel them; it also appears that animals are quite sensitive to them, and will sometimes refuse to go near some stones where strong energy lines are flowing.. On the CEMG visit to the Lizard peninsula in Sept 1997 the group went to Tremenhir standing stone [SW7777 2103], but as they walked across the field to the stone, a dog who was with one of the group stopped dead in his tracks and refused to go an inch further, despite being pulled and coaxed. When the Group dowsed the point, they all found a very strong energy line running parallel to the stone. Nobody had been aware of it until they dowsed, but the dog knew!

However, despite all this (anecdotal) evidence, we seem to be no nearer to the meaning of these lines. The nub of the problem is a chicken and egg situation: are they natural currents set off by electro-magnetic, water or radiation energy in the earth, that ancient peoples could tap in to, and build their monuments on, or were they created by the movement of peoples from those monuments across the land, perhaps moving in a ritualised way from one site to another? There is some evidence for both interpretations: the fact is that sites were often located over underground blind springs, or natural ducts and fissures in the earth (it has been claimed that every stone circle in Britain lies less than a mile from a geological fault). But also, we know from other native peoples, such as the Australian aborigines, that they walk particular ritual paths across the land from one natural feature to another (such as particular rocks and trees), often singing sacred songs as they go. These 'song lines' then become established on the ground after a period of time. They may be invisible to the western eye, but the Aboriginal people can see and sense these lines. They have made a physical imprint on the Land. It is not too fanciful to suggest that ancient peoples in Britain did the same as they walked from one sacred site to another.

Some sites seem to lend themselves to this kind of 'sacred line'. For example, the archaeologist John Barnatt has suggested that such a sacred line, or 'processional way' ran from the Nine Maidens Boskednan stone circle [SW4343 3512] to the rocky outcrop ('holy hill') of Carn Galva. This line or way is marked by two tall pillars in the circle, and flanked by a number of barrows and a standing stone along the route. Another similar 'processional way' runs from The Hurlers stone circles on Bodmin Moor [SX2584 7146] via Rillaton Barrow [SX2603 7191] to Stowe's Hill and the distinctive shape of the Cheesewring. There may be many other such sacred routes running from ancient sites if we start to look, for example from Tregeseal Circle [SW3866 3238] to the distinctive rocky outcrop of Carn Kenidjack on the horizon, or from Stannon Circle on Bodmin Moor [SX1257 8010] to the very distinctive Rough Tor, or from the Trippet Stones circle on Bodmin Moor [SX1312 7501] to the hill above, crowned by the Stripple Stones circle [SX1312 7501]. All these may be a special kind of ritual pathway, that is now dowseable as an energy line.

So, "energy lines" may indeed be 'real' and able to be dowsed and walked. They may well have existed, or been created, at the time of the megalith builders, and the placing of their sites in the Land may owe something to the existence of these lines. There are, however, other curious things going on at many of these ancient sites, and it is to these anomalous energies that we now turn our attention.

Processional way from Nine Maidens stone circle to Carn Galva

15

Chapter 3 – Hot Spots at the Ancient Sites
Radiation and its effects

Many strange and unexplained effects have been reported from time to time at ancient sites, so much so that a specific project The Dragon Project was set up in the 1980s to investigate these anomalies.[9] There was some research at sites in Cornwall, and this work was carried on by the Cornish Earth Mysteries Group (CEMG) after it was founded in 1990. These anomalies are of three main types: Radiation, Magnetism, and Ultrasound.

RADIATION

Although the term 'radiation' has become associated with the fall-out from nuclear explosions, and is therefore known to have a devastating effect on the human body, the earth, and all the creatures who live on her, are constantly affected by natural radiation. This comes from two sources: from outer space the earth is bombarded with cosmic rays, which interact with molecules in the upper atmosphere and cause secondary particles of radiation. And some minerals that constitute the earth herself are also radioactive, in particular, uranium, thorium and potassium-40. Granite is a particularly radioactive rock, one of the products of its decay (half-life) being the natural gas radon, which cannot be seen or smelt, but in large quantities in an enclosed space can be cancer-inducing. Granite is particularly prevalent in Cornwall, and the levels of background radiation some of the highest in Britain. Paul Devereux has pointed out[10] that it may or may not be a coincidence that Cornwall has one of the highest, if not *the* highest, concentrations of megaliths in Britain. Is there a connection here? Were more megalithic sites built in Cornwall, because the builders were somehow aware of the radiation levels (though as radon is undetectable it is difficult to see how)? Or is it simply that because Cornwall has been predominantly rural and remote from the rest of Britain, at least until the 19th Century, that more megaliths were preserved there than anywhere else?

The first step in determining any causal link between radiation levels and the megaliths is to measure the radiation at the sites. Some work has been done to do just this, using a variety of geiger counter devices, some

---

[9] See Paul Devereux *Places of Power* [Blandford, 1990]
[10] Ibid. P.61

professionally made and some put together by knowledgeable individuals. It is actually not difficult to build a device that can measure radioactive emissions as counts-per-minute (cpm), and the CEMG had such a device built for them by someone from Cambridge University. The Dragon project themselves had several professional instruments, and the results that follow are a combination of research results from both Dragon & CEMG.

The earliest monuments to be built in Cornwall from the Neolithic period were the dolmens, sometimes called cromlechs, or in Cornwall, quoits. The purpose of these monuments is still debated by archaeologists, but it does appear that they were not simply burial places for the dead, but sacred monuments to which the living would go to connect with the spirits of the dead. Of the Quoits that have been looked at in Cornwall, Trethevy Quoit [SX2594 6881], north of Liskeard on the flanks of Bodmin Moor, was found to have a higher radiation count than background. In fact, the enclosed inner chamber, when measured with three different radiation counters in July 1988, was found to be 103% higher than background.

Trethevy Quoit

17

A similar count was found at Chûn Quoit [SW4023 3396], where the inner chamber there showed a 123% higher reading than background. Also at Tregiffian Barrow in West Penwith [SW4304 2442]. Inside Tregiffian Barrow there was found a very high reading of 160-180 cpm in 1988 compared with 75-80 cpm background (210% above average). One wonders if the high radiation readings inside these enclosed chambers could be connected in any way with the suggested use of the cromlech and barrows as places where the shamans and shamankas of the tribe would go on spirit journeys to connect with the spirits of the dead and the ancestors. This is a topic to which we shall return shortly.

After the Quoits, the next monuments to be constructed in the late Neolithic and the early Bronze Age were the stone circles. Some of these have measured for radiation levels. And here, we have seen the *opposite* effect to that of the Quoits. Four sites have been checked. In 1982 Alan Bleakley[11] checked Stannon Circle [SX1257 8010]on Bodmin Moor and was amazed to find that his geiger counter was completely silent for a prolonged period of time inside the circle. He was able to confirm that it was not instrument failure, and that readings could be obtained in the countryside around. After a while, readings began again, and the anomaly was never explained.

Stannon Circle

---

[11] See Paul Devereux *Places of Power* [Blandford, 1990] p.166-7

Bleakley also checked the stone circle at Nine Maidens Boskednan in West Penwith [SW4343 3512], which produced a count of 12 cpm in the circle against the average Cornish background of 30 cpm. The site was checked on four separate occasions, and every time produced site averages below background. Tregeseal Circle [SW3866 3238] was also checked by CEMG in 1991 and the centre of the circle was measured as slightly below background. The Merry Maidens in West Penwith [SW4237 2451] has been checked on at least four separate occasions, and, with one exception, was found to be lower than average in the circle. The exception was the first set of readings taken by Bleakley in 1982, which found a *higher* than average reading in the centre, but this is the only such anomaly reported at any of the stone circle sites in Cornwall. Subsequently, the Merry Maidens were checked again in 1985 by Don Robins, who found that geiger readings halved when he moved inside the circle of stones. In 1988 the site was checked twice. Readings were taken up to 400 yds east and west of the circle, and inside the circle, and a small, but significant, fall from background was confirmed.

It seems that, unlike the enclosed spaces of dolmens and burial chambers, the open spaces of stone circles have low radiation. But why should this be so? We might expect that the readings would be the same as background, or else slightly higher, as the circle of granite stones might accentuate the radiation effect. One possible explanation offered is that if the site were cleared of soil when the stone circle was first erected, radioactive zircons would be removed and subsequent replacement of the soil would not create more. But if so, why would this be happening only at stone circles, and not at other kinds of sites? It is as if the effect of the stones in a circle produced some kind of 'ring of power' that circulated around the stones and absorbed the natural radiation as well, leaving the centre of the circle free from radiation and acting as a kind of 'sanctuary' area. If ancient peoples were aware of this effect in some way, it may be that the circles were built deliberately as places of protection and safety.

This theory is given some credence by Boscawen-ûn Circle [SW4122 2736] in West Penwith. This site was checked by CEMG in 1992. The stones themselves had high counts (average 18 cpm) compared to a background of 12 cpm. Once again, the centre of the circle was lower (12 cpm) though not significantly lower than background. But the real surprise here was that the distinctive quartz stone in the circle (the only one out of 19) had much lower readings than the other 18 stones and the centre stone. The quartz stone has often been considered to be the healing stone of the circle, and, if this were the case in antiquity as well, perhaps the stone was felt to have a calming and restful effect on whoever touched or stroked it.

There is one other stone circle in Cornwall that is also composed of quartz stones – Duloe circle [SX2359 5830] that lies between Liskeard and Looe, and which, interestingly, has also been observed to be a 'sanctuary' site, as cows from the field, where the circle stands, were seen deliberately going into the circle in order to give birth.[12] Animals are often intuitively in touch with the 'energies' present at these kind of sites, as we have already seen.

Duloe Circle

The Mên-an-Tol holed stone, which stands on the West Penwith moors between Madron and Morvah [SW4264 3493], was built about the same time as the stone circles: indeed it well may have been originally a part of a stone circle This too has been tested for radiation, and the inside edges of the hole found to be at a level about double that of background. It has been suggested[13] that a short sharp dose of radiation, received by passing a child through the hole, might act in some kind of homeopathic way. Hence the legend attached to the stone that if you pass a child through 3 (or 9) times it will be cured of rickets. This is not as fanciful as it might seem, when we think of radiation therapy that is used today in cancer treatment.

---

[12] see 'Duloe Circle – a healing sanctuary' *Lee Elston-Jenkins* [Meyn Mamvro12, p.15.
[13] by Paul Devereux in *Places of Power* [Blandford, 1990] p.188

20

Some thousand years or so after the last of the stone circles were built, the inhabitants of Cornwall were living in Courtyard House settlements and building so-called 'cliff castles' and 'hill forts'. These were the Iron Age Celtic peoples who flourished from about 800 BCE- 500 CE, and the most distinctive – and enigmatic – monument that they have left us is the Fogou. These underground curved chambers, often with side passages and creeps, were built all over West Cornwall. They were constructed out of alternate layers of organic and inorganic material, and consist primarily of large granite stones. Their purpose is still really unknown, but of the three possible explanations: refuge, storage or ceremony, it is the latter theory, their ritual use, that has found most favour. Today many of the sites continue to be used by the pagan community of west Cornwall for ritual and ceremony, and some strange effects have been reported in them at various times [see Ch.11 for more details].

The three best-preserved fogous in West Penwith, Pendeen, Carn Euny and Boleigh, have all been checked for radiation readings. The interior of Pendeen [SW3837 3553] was measured at about the same as Trethevy Quoit (above), at some 91% higher than the local exterior background; Carn Euny [SW4024 2885] was 87% higher than background, which itself was very high; and Boleigh [SW4370 2520] was higher even than Chûn Quoit, its relative level being double that of the (high) exterior background. These readings led Paul Devereux to conclude: "I believe the Cornish fogous were yet another structural design created in prehistory to make opportunistic use of the radioactive properties of the environment."[14]

Finally, we come to the holy wells of Cornwall. No one is sure when these were first constructed, but people must have visited these 'sacred shrines' well back into prehistory. The well surrounds, mostly made of granite, that now exist around many of the springs were probably originally constructed in the early Christian period, from about 5th-8th century CE, but many of them have been rebuilt and restored over the years. In Cornwall, just two wells have been checked for radiation readings: Madron Baptistry well [SW4465 3280], and Sancreed Well [SW4180 2935], but both gave startling results. At Madron, the Chapel itself, being made of granite, was of course higher than background. But the water in the well-basin, measured by floating counters on it, had the highest readings of all, over double that of the environment, and 49% higher than the

---

[14] Paul Devereux *Places of Power* [Blandford, 1990] p.151

21

interior of the chapel. And Sancreed Well, which consists of steps leading down right into the well chamber inside the earth, registered the highest radiation counts anywhere in Cornwall, nearly 200% overall above background. With one instrument, readings off the surface of the water itself were regularly in the order of three times or more than those found in the exterior background!

Sancreed Well

So what does this all mean? It seems that ancient sites with enclosed spaces, such as Quoits, Burial Chambers, Fogous and Holy Wells have very high radiation levels; conversely, more open sites, such as stone circles, have in their interior relatively low levels. We can measure all this with our modern instrumentation, but the question is, were the ancient peoples, who built these places, aware of these phenomena? There is some evidence that they may have been. A Czech scientist Dr.Zaboj V.Harvalik carried out controlled tests in America with dowsers, and became convinced that some skilled dowsers could be more sensitive to weak amounts of radioactivity than geiger counters. But perhaps it was not the radioactivity itself that was only noticed by the megalithic builders, but some of its associated affects, such as the propensity of people to go into a languorous state in an enclosed space with high radiation[15], and even for it to induce altered states of consciousness. This is something we shall explore in the future chapters, along with the phenonema of magnetism.

---

[15] Paul Devereux observed this happen at Sancreed Well. In *Places of Power* p.157 he says: "The prime energy effect of the place is the sense of calm it engenders. Peace. Repose. I have actually seen every person in a group of 15 people enter a deep, languid state, here , or completely fall asleep. It is a place to sleep; to have the Dream of Earth".

Chapter 4 – Magnetic Mysteries
Magnetism and human consciousness

MAGNETISM

The Earth itself is a giant magnet. Movement in the earth's core (which consists of solid iron-rich alloy surrounded by a fluid outer core of molten iron sulphide) creates a magnetic field, which is detectable with magnetic compasses. Compasses point (in the northern hemisphere) to the magnetic north pole (which differs from both true, i.e geographical north, and grid north by a few varying degrees each year). The earth's magnetic poles have not always been where they are now: for reasons that they are still not really understood the poles reverse themselves every 100,000 years or so. We are in fact overdue for a reversal now, in which the North magnetic pole will become the South magnetic pole, and vice-versa. However, the prehistoric period we are considering, when Britain and Cornwall was first inhabited is, at most, 6000 years ago, so the magnetic poles were certainly in their current orientation then..

Although one might expect that where ever you go, your compass needle will point to magnetic north, in fact this is not always the case. Some rocks and stones that are rich in iron-bearing minerals, such as lodestone, seem to show higher magnetic 'charges' than other sedimentary rocks. A famous case in point is Carn Ingli in the Prescili Hills in south Wales, which displays considerable magnetic anomalies, and, interestingly, is reputed in legend to be the place of visions and madness, as well as being the source of the bluestones that were transported to Stonehenge. Ancient peoples seem to have been aware of the special 'power' of this place. The question is, were they also aware of other spots on the earth that had similar qualities, or other stones that displayed similar properties, and if so, did they deliberately site their megalithic monuments at these places, or build them with these stones?

Some research has been done on sites in Cornwall, and, while it should be stressed that in most cases no significant anomalies were found, nevertheless there are a few recorded examples that give pause for thought. One of these is the Nine Stones circle near Altarnun on Bodmin Moor [SX2361 7815]. While surveying the circle in the 1980s, archaeologist John Barnatt was occasionally interrupted by groups of Royal Marines on an orienteering and route march exercise coming to the site, taking compass bearings and then departing.

Nine Stones, Altarnun circle

John Barnatt says: "As I observed them using maps and compass to work out their next destination, I gradually noticed that they frequently set off on strange headings – often 60 degrees out of line. I put this down to their inability to read maps. Later in the day I mentioned this in conversation with one of the officers who were supervising the exercise when he happened to call at the site. He told me that they had chosen the stone circles because in the past they had observed magnetic anomalies at these, which created an added test of the cadets' ability to read maps!"[16]

Another site that has shown some compass deflections is the Merry Maidens near Lamorna in West Penwith [SW4327 2451]. It was checked by the CEMG in Summer 1991, when some stones did appear to marginally deflect the compass readings. This was confirmed by the Knights Rose team headed by Hamish Miller who detected a 30° magnetic anomaly in the north of the circle.[17] The site was also checked with the Dragon Project magnetometer in Summer 1991. This measures the site against the earth's magnetic field. Results at the stones varied between 25-28µt to 45µt against the normal British field strength of 47µt, but the low figures may possibly have been the result of sampling error.

---

[16] Paul Devereux *Places of Power* [Blandford, 1990] p.179
[17] *The Spirit of the Serpent* video [Knights Rose, 2003]

However, it is interesting to note that it was at this circle that Hamish Miller experienced a "violent electric shock" from one of the stones[18] The granite stones in Cornwall all have a high quartz content, and quartz is known to have a piezo-electric effect (it is used to power watches). Touching stones raises the internal pressure and gives off minute charges of electrical potential difference, the cause of the tingles and electric shocks experienced by Hamish and others at the stones. This peiezo-electric effect could also be linked to the magnetism and be part of the same electro-magnetic phenomenon of the stones.

The other piece of anecdotal evidence concerns Boscawen-ûn circle [SW4122 2736]. In 1994 I gave a talk to the St.Just Old Cornwall Society on Earth Mysteries, and one of the audience was a surveyor with South West Water who told me that he was surveying in the area of the farm some years earlier. While doing some compass measurements in the circle itself, he had experienced total compass disorientation, which had really thrown him. These are only a few examples, but there may be others at other sites. Very few sites have been checked in detail, which is something anyone can do with the time and patience and the use of a hand-held compass.

Once again the question is – were the site builders aware of these magnetic anomalies in the local rocks or in the stones which they chose for their sites? Sensitivity to the earth's magnetic fields is in fact quite well attested in a number of different species. It has long been thought that birds navigate over thousands of miles by a combination of watching the skies and responding to the earth's magnetic forces. Researchers have also found that certain bacteria, snails and worms, honey bees and even mice are able to detect incredibly weak magnetic fields. And in the seas, algae, crabs, salamander, salmon, tuna and other sea creatures have been shown in different experiments to be able to respond to the earth's magnetic forces. Recent research has also shown that whales and dolphins seem able to cruise along 'magnetic stripes' laid out on the ocean floors due to tectonic activity.

There has also been some research on human beings. Dr.Harvalik carried out research on dowsers in Virginia, USA, and was able to prove that they were able to achieve incredible amounts of sensitivity to magnetism. Magnetometric measurements indicate that a dowser reacts to magnetic gradient

---

[18] Hamish Miller *Dowsing the Earth's Energies* [Meyn Mamvro no.5 p.3-5]

changes as weak as one millimicrogauss. The earth's field strength is about half a gauss, so this is about 0.000000005 times smaller than that! It is thus perfectly feasible that ancient peoples would have been able to detect changes in the earth's magnetic field, especially if, as has been suggested, the strength of the earth's magnetic field was greater then.

How did this work? It has been shown that in many creatures sensitive to magnetic changes, small grains of magnetite have been found, as if they are carrying their own biological compass. In the early 1980s experiments carried out by Dr. Robin Baker of Manchester University detected a thin embedded layer of high iron content in the bones forming the walls of the sinuses, the deep complex in close proximity to parts of the brain. We are beginning to form a picture of the people who built the megalithic sites being intuitively connected to forces of the earth, like radiation, magnetism, underground water lines, cosmic energies, etc. This idea underlies Serena Roney-Dougal's book *Where Science and Magic Meet.*[19] She points out that the effect of the earth's magnetic field on human consciousness, and says: "In other words, because many of the British stone circles are built on quartz-bearing granite intrusions, and are themselves built out of ancient quartz-bearing stone, the whole circle is surrounded by unusual geomagnetic fields, and static electric, sonic and infrared discharges occur when such activity as dawn, or hand pressure, touches the stones".

She points out that the complexity of a magnetic anomaly map is very often indicative of the geological complexity of an area, so that the west coast of Britain – Cornwall, Wales, Cumbria and Scotland – are all areas of both intense geological faulting and magnetic anomalies. "These are the very areas where you get the majority of the ancient sites, ley lines, UFO sightings and people with 'second sight'" But why would these forces of magnetism and electromagnetic energies have been so important to them? The answer may lie in the realm of healing and divination.

It is noticeable that many of the ancient sites have legends of divination associated with them. A case in point is the Mên-an-Tol. As well as the healing legend recounted in Ch.3, there is also a legend here that if a brass pin is placed on the top of the holed stone, the direction it swings will give the answer to any

---

[19] Serena Roney-Dougal *Where Science and Magic Meet* [Element, 1991]

question. This may be a reference to some magnetic anomalies at the site, for it is the interaction between the magnetic (or radioactive) properties of a site and human consciousness that gives insight into the realm of the unconscious, wherein are contained the answers to many of the questions of which our conscious minds are unaware. In addition at this site, there is the legend of a piskey guardian who could perform cures. Janet Bord has speculated that electro-magnetic energy at places like this may cause certain people to see fairies and other elementals, the fairy image being an externalisation of the fairy image stored within our collective memories.[20]

Mên-an-Tol: site of healing, divination and otherworld legends

The connection between electromagnetism and brain wave activity is documented. Paul Devereux comments: "It is known that the temporal lobe area of the brain is sensitive to electromagnetism, and parts of it, such as the hippocampus, are related to dreaming and to memory. Magnetic fields can stimulate these parts of the brain, and can produce in the subject sensations of floating, even out-of-the body sensations, the production of vivid hallucinatory images into waking consciousness, and mystical and visionary states. It has also been discovered that the human head produces a weak magnetic field of its own.

---

[20] Janet Bord *Fairies – Real encounters with Little People* [Michael O'Mara Books, 1997]

Perhaps this field can act as a kind of interface between the brain and variable magnetic fields in the environment."[21]

Perhaps this is what happened at the Merry Maidens stone circle, where, as has already been noted, a large magnetic variation was found. Could this be behind the legends of the stones "dancing" around the fields, which is linked to the story of the nineteen dancing maidens? Perhaps the electromagnetic energy emitted from the stones in an unusual or anomalous pattern can affect the consciousness of those in contact with the stones, and under certain conditions, allow for visionary or trance states.

The same thing may have happened at Carn Gluze (Ballowal) that stands on the cliff edge outside St.Just in West Penwith [SW3555 3124]. Fairies are associated with this site as well, and there is a tradition of miners having seen fairies dancing around the site in the 19th century. This area stands on a geological fault line, and there are the remains of much mining activity around the barrow, so it would not be surprising if there had been disturbance of the minerals and rocks where the barrow stands, with corresponding geomagnetic stresses. It is almost as if the earth's activity (or activity into the earth) 'releases' the fairies, or dancing maidens, themselves, and brings them into human consciousness by a wave of electromagnetic energy.

Carn Gluze (Balowall) Barrow, where the fairies dance.

---

[21] Paul Devereux *Places of Power* [Blandford, 1990] p.207

Chapter 5 – The Sound of the Earth's Song
Ultrasound, Infrasound & the Hummadruz

ULTRASOUND

The upper limit at which human beings can hear sound is usually around 20 kHz. Certain other creatures can hear sounds above this range, in particular bats who emit ultrasonic squeaks for echo-location purposes at frequencies above 100 kHz, and dolphins who emit ultrasound noises from their larynx for echo-location and probably communication, at frequencies up to 200 kHz. As far as we know, there is nothing in the natural world to produce such sounds. And yet, the Dragon Project detected ultrasound noise at the Rollright Stone Circle in Oxfordshire at dawn and sunset on a number of occasions.

Using an ultrasound detector, some stone circles in West Penwith were checked by the CEMG in 1991/2. At the Merry Maidens [SW4237 2451] nothing significant was found, and the same at Boscawen-ûn [SW4122 2736], although a recumbent stone to the east of the circle did produce some clicks and bangs. More work needs to be done in this field, especially at dawn and sunset.

Ultrasound testing at the Quartz Stone at Boscawen-ûn

If there is anything significant going on at the megaliths, how would the sound be produced? Don Robins has suggested[22] that microwave energy from the rising sun might energize electrons held in energy traps inside a stone's atomic lattice. The pressure wave would then manifest as ultrasound.

If ancient peoples were aware of this effect, how might it have been used? We know nowadays that ultrasound can be used for healing, and is used in modern medicine. If the megalithic builders were able to harness or tap into this effect at stone circles at certain times, might they have been able to use the sites for healing purposes? Much more work needs to be done in this field, but there are certainly some intriguing possibilities.

INFRASOUND
The lower limit at which human beings can hear sound is usually around 20 Hz. Some individuals can detect tones below this, down to a low of 7-5 Hz, but there can be unpleasant side effects, such as nausea, dizziness, lethargy and an inability to concentrate. When an individual is exposed to low infrasound (such as with machinery, office vibrations, etc) these effects will manifest, even if they cannot 'hear' the noise. However, low noise vibration may also have been used by the megalithic builders to create special effects. Some work has been done on specific sites, such as the Hypogeum in Malta, Newgrange in Ireland, and Maes Howe on Orkney, which shows that the sites may have been deliberately constructed to create low-audible sounds that could resonate and help to induce trance states in celebrants there. It was noticeable that during a CEMG visit to Halligye Fogou on the Lizard in 1992, a didgeridoo that was blown into the small passage by Andy Tanner resonated around the chamber and helped to create the conditions for the 'imaging' work that was to follow.

There has also been some checking of sites in Cornwall. In 1994 an inter-disciplinary research group, the International Consciousness Research Laboratories (ICRL) tested the acoustical resonances of several megalithic sites in Britain, including two in Cornwall.[23] One of these was Chûn Quoit [SW4023 3396], already mentioned in connection with the high radiation count [Ch.3] and the energy line running through it [Ch.2]. The composite resonance frequency of the Quoit was found to be 110Hz, which is at the low end of

---

[22] Don Robins *Circles of Silence* [Souvenir Press, 1985]
[23] Paul Devereux *Stone Age Soundtracks* [Vega, 2001] p.81-2

30

human voice emission. They also checked the Beehive Hut at Carn Euny fogou [SW4024 2885], which was found to be similarly low at 99Hz. Low-voice chanting, both male and female, works extremely powerfully at this site. Both here and at Carn Euny fogou, there have been other associated phenomena relating to altered states of consciousness, as we shall see in Ch.11.

As well as the research done at these sites, there are is an anecdotal incident that has been reported from a site in Cornwall that seems to relate to infrasound. It occured at the Blind Fiddler menhir near St.Buryan in West Penwith [SW4252 2818], where in June 1987 at the Summer Solstice, two people, Michael Woolf and Rachel Garcia experienced what could be described literally as the 'Earth's song'.

Sunset at the Blind Fiddler standing stone

They described it thus:-
"We entered the field, to find ourselves alone but for the long-eared crop whispering in the slight breeze. Touching the menhir, we looked west to see the sun edging along the hills, steadily losing height. We noticed a clearly visible notch in one hill, and from where we stood, it almost seemed that this notch had been created to drain the last drops of sunlight into the earth at midsummer.

Moments later, the mist began to return, but not before our answer came. The sun obligingly slipped into the notch on the western hill and disappeared from view. There was a momentary stillness – and then came the 'earth-thunder'. It was like a sudden, muffled thunderclap, audible but emanating from beneath the earth. It did not shake the ground, but seemed to alter the air pressure, the way explosions do. We are convinced that the sound emanated from within the earth, as if a charge was triggered, perhaps by certain alignments between the earth and her sister spheres. Could the stones act to amplify these signals?"[24]

Whatever the sound was, or from whence it came, similar sounds have been reported by other people in other places. If our ancestors heard similar sounds, might they not have attributed it to the voice of Mother Earth herself?

THE HUMMADRUZ

Another strange sound phenonema is that of the Hummadruz. This is a word coined in the 19th century for an enigmatic low humming noise, heard in the country, usually in still summer weather, and with no apparent source. On a CEMG visit to Zennor Quoit [SW4688 3801] and Trendrine Hill on July 6th 1997, several members of the Group heard it, and it was subsequently reported by Andy Norfolk in an article in *Meyn Mamvro*.[25]:

"It was a glorious sunny day with a cloudless sky and no wind. We walked up to the Quoit and when we got there it was quite quiet with no noise, except a lot of chatter. Most of us walked on to Sperris Quoit and then to the top of Trendrine Hill where there is a trig. point at 247m above sea level. Carol, who stayed on her own at Zennor Quoit, heard a loud humming or buzzing noise as if there were large numbers of bees or other insects flying around, but there were hardly any to be seen. Dionne, who walked to Trendrine Hill, was very aware of all this noise all the time we were on the top of the downs. There were a few light aircraft flying nearby at various times but very little traffic noise. Although there were a few insects, they were noticeable as they flew by as distinct from the background noise. Dionne and I walked back to collect Carol from Zennor Quoit and all three of us heard the noise very clearly. It was quite different from the aircraft noises. Carol and I have kept bees in the past and the noise was very like a contented hive but there were no bees nearby. The noise was all around and it was impossible to locate a source. There seemed to be no

---

[24] M.Woolf & R.Garcia *Sunset with the Blind Fiddler* [Meyn Mamvro no.4]
[25] Andy Norfolk *The Hummadruz at Zennor Quoit* [Meyn Mamvro no.35]

difference between the noise in badly burnt areas and those where the heather was in flower. As we walked down off the top of the downs the noise faded away, disappearing as we got below approximately the 200m contour, to be replaced with the more usual noise of crickets and other insects – quite different."

CEMG at Zennor Quoit, location of the Hummadruz

This Hummadruz sound, or one similar to it, has been reported by other people at other places, and Andy Norfolk's article gives other examples. Philip Heselton in *Earth Mysteries*[26] suggested that such sounds may have been used to help induce altered states of consciousness. The authors of the book *Earthmind*[27] suggest that in certain mental states our brainwaves are resonating with the rhythms of the Earth, and say that activity in the hippocampus in the brain is affected by electromagnetic stimulation, with the largest effect at the 'earth frequency' of 10-15 Hz. Alpha and theta brainwaves are encouraged by noises and sounds that resonate at low frequencies, and these brainwaves are associated with visionary and paranormal experiences. They suggest that in certain states we can directly open up to "the vast ocean of biological-frequency natural forces of the planet." Interestingly, the area where the CEMG members walked (from Zennor Quoit to Trendrine Hill and back) is a well-attested 'ley line' that runs all the way across the Penwith moors to Boswens menhir.

---

[26] Philip Heselton *Earth Mysteries* [Element, 1991]
[27] Paul Devereux, John Steele & David Kubrin *Earthmind* [Harper & Row, 1989]

In Serena Roney-Dougal's book *Where Science and Magic Meet.*[28],she says that some noises associated with electrostatic phenomena, such as clicks, swishing and hisses, are likely to be the effects of electromagnetic energy impinging on the eardrum and being heard as noises. She also notes the correlations between ancient monuments, electromagnetic anomalies, UFO sightings, fairy lore and geological faulting. She draws attention to the sounds of rushing water that Thomas the Rhymer hears constantly in the old folk tale as he travels to the otherworld. In the Cornish tale by Robert Hunt of a "covetous old man of St.Just" who hears beautiful music and sees fairy revels on the Gump[29], Hunt says that the old man was about to use his hat to cover the fairy table when he heard a shrill whistle and everything went dark. "Whir! Whir! Whir! As if a flight of bees were passing him, buzzed in his ears. Every limb from head to foot was as if stuck full of pins and pinched with tweazers." We seem to be back with the Hummadruz again.

There have been many other examples of this Hummadruz being heard in Cornwall. In particular, it seems to be centered in a triangular area of land covering Hayle, Penzance and Praa Sands. Following a TV programme on the phenomena by Westcountry TV in 1997, a correspondent who was an engineer wrote to the *Western Morning News* suggesting that the hum has a low note between 15-20Hz, together with a higher note less than 40 HZ, and sometimes a third harmonic of just over 50Hz. Following on from Andy Norfolk's article in *Meyn Mamvro,* other readers wrote in with their experiences of Hummadruz noises.[30] Firstly, Barry and Kate Reilly of Sancreed:

"On the afternoon of the earthquake in West Cornwall (Nov 10th 1996) we went for a walk up on Caer Bran (an Iron Age hillfort). We were quite near to the part where the quarry curves round when we heard this 'buzzing' or 'humming' sound coming from the gorse bushes, about a yard away from us. We walked towards it to see what was causing it and the sound moved away, about another yard. Again, we walked towards it and again it moved away. I wondered if it was anything to do with electricity, as the sound resembled that produced by the 1930s movies, just at the point where Frankenstein's monster is being revived, but I could see no electrical equipment of any sort around. Not wishing to go

---

[28] Serena Roney-Dougal *Where Science and Magic Meet* [Element, 1991]
[29] Robert Hunt *Popular Romances of the West of England* [1871]
[30] *Strange sounds – and lights* [Meyn Mamvro no.36]

into the gorse bushes any further, we gave up and concluded that it was a large group of very shy grasshoppers!"

Grasshoppers notwithstanding, what we have here is a very useful account, particularly as it is linked to the earthquake, which was quite a large one, measuring 3.6 on the Richter scale. The second account is also very intriguing, and comes from Sue Aston, now living in Cornwall.

"I was looking forward to exploring Warleggan Church on Bodmin Moor, as I had read an article describing the bizarre lifestyle of the Rev. Densham. We had had an inspiring day which saw us take in Roche Rock, the Hurlers, St.Cleer and Dozmary Pool. However, nothing could have prepared me for what I was about to experience at Warleggan. We walked up the hill to the Church and a sense of apprehension descended upon us. As I entered the Church immediately experienced the crushing atmosphere of the place. To begin with I thought I was going to faint, although I was feeling perfectly well and alert, but I could not understand the rushing noise in my ears. I swallowed hard, expecting my ears to pop, but still the noise persisted. The sound was almost electronic in a way – as though there was a motor boat droning away under the floor. As I looked around the church, I remember feeling a sense that something powerful was present there with us – it was a most disarming experience.

Still this noise persisted and apparently only I could hear it – and it was so loud. I found it incredible that people had written in the visitors' book comments describing the Church as 'beautiful and peaceful' – it was anything but to me! I was relieved to get outside, and noticed at once that the noise in my ears stopped! I have since read about the phenomenon known as 'the singing' or Hummadruz. Paul Broadhurst mentions it in his book *Secret Shrines*[31] and says that it can occur on moors and in old churches. I would be most interested to know if anyone else has experienced it at Warleggan before, and what it signifies. Is it earth energy or the past events at the Church which triggered off this Hummadruz?"

The question is a good one, and the account particularly interesting because it shows that the effect of the Hummadruz on human consciousness. Perhaps the answer is that it is not one or the other but both: the effect of the

---

[31] Paul Broadhurst *Secret Shrines* [Pendragon Press, 1988]

low frequency noise triggering a psychic reaction in which a very old atmospheric place like Warleggan 'releases' some of the memory of old events and emotions that linger there.

Warleggan Church – scene of a Hummadruz encounter

Another experience of the phenomenon happened to Rod Blunsdon at the Merry Maidens stone circle [SW4237 2451] at midnight on a starlit night, around the mid-1990s. There was some anomalous light phenomena [see Ch.6] and then the people there heard strange voices, speaking words in a language he did not understand, together with humming and singing. In 1995 the CEMG visited Halligye fogou [SW7132 2395] for an imaging session [see Ch.11] and heard a loud and continuous chirruping sound for the duration of the mediatation, which ended abruptly when the session ended. However, perhaps the final word on all of this should go to the late Jean Harris, who wrote:
"I have been hearing this humming noise since childhood, growing up in the far west of Penwith. It is one of those mysterious phenomena of which I have always been aware, but never tried to analyse, any more than the tappings and clicks heard in houses where I have lived. I believe that hearing the Hummadruz can defy logical explanations and just "is", as if the Otherworld, at times, on a still summer day or a moonlit night, unfolds its boundaries and entices us with a subliminal experience from another dimension. Personally, I have usually found that hearing these strange noises are synonymous with some significant spiritual encounter."

Chapter 6   Light on the Earth's Mysteries
Strange lights at the sites

Strange inexplicable lights have been reported from time to time at ancient sites. For example, in 1991 Craig Weatherhill photographed Treen Common circle/enclosure in West Penwith [SW4446 3666] at sunset. When the photographs were developed, one only revealed some parallel shafts of light appearing to come out from or go into one of the stones. Craig said that it was neither a fault in the camera nor on the film. Similar anomalous lights have been photographed elsewhere: Don Rowe took a photo of the NE Piper standing stone [SW4354 2482] in mid-afternoon during a ley walk around the area in July 1990, and when it was developed a strange light appeared to be emanating out of the side of the stone. And I took a number of photographs of Mulfra Quoit [SW4518 3536] in 1986. When they were developed, all were perfect except one that showed a strange blue light coming out of the stones.

Strange lights at Mulfra Quoit

Another photograph of an inexplicable light was taken in the late 1980s at the Rocky Valley maze carvings near Tintagel in North Cornwall [SX0715 8940]. This site is supposedly Bronze Age, though, judging by the cutting of the labyrinths in the rock face and the similarities to ones in Ireland, a Celtic Iron-

Age date is much more likely. Whatever the age, the maze or labyrinth is an ancient sacred symbol, and the carvings at Rocky Valley are much visited.

Labyrinth carvings at Rocky Valley

Jo Pacsoo was one of those who visited the site, and she tells the story in her own words:[32]
"I sat for a while on the hillside just beyond the (old Mill) ruins and felt that here was a magical spot, a deep and potent stillness. Returning to the carvings, I remembered reading that these were originally used to induce trance states by tracing the shape with a finger; and I did this too. The rock was certainly very smooth, as if from the rubbing of many fingers, and it required concentration to follow the curves. I traced the way in and out several times and was beginning to get into the rhythm of it when my friend called to me, and as I looked up he took a photograph with my finger still on the carving. Two months later, when this film was developed, I was surprised to see a reddish band right across the picture coming off my elbow in line with the finger touching the carving. If light had got into the camera, that would usually make a fuzzy area at the edge, not a beam right across the middle, and it does not appear on any of the other photos. Perhaps it is in some way connected with the carving and my action in tracing it? If the film has picked up some 'energy' from the carvings, then the magic of Rocky Valley is still available".

---

[32] Jo Pacsoo *Meanness and Magic in Cornwall* [Meyn Mamvro no.19, p.4]

The strange light at Rocky Valley mazes

Someone else who experienced a strange light energy at a site was LH of St.Just. She went to Boscawen-ûn stone circle [SW4122 2736] for the first time, and as she was going around the stones and put her hands on one of them, she was struck with a blinding light. She comments: "It engulfed me with love, wonderful intense love". She then heard her companions voice talking to her, which she says brought her back to normal.

Two other strange light experiences occurred at the Merry Maidens stone circle in West Penwith [SW4327 2451]. Firstly, in the mid 1980s in the month of July Rod Blunsdon was at the circle at midnight with a friend at midnight on a starlight night with no moon. Between them they had 3 cameras: on one camera he had taken 3 photographs with inbuilt flash on the way to the circle and it had worked perfectly. Outside the circle itself, the flash also worked OK, but subsequently it was revealed that no photographs taken there came out. However, it was inside the circle that strange things really began to happen. No flashes on any of the cameras would work, and subsequently when the films were developed, there were no pictures except on one of them, which, despite the lack of flash, showed pictures of Rod illuminated from the feet up with a brilliant white light. Also in the photograph were revealed anomalous BOLs (balls of light) floating around in front of the stones. These BOLs have appeared on other photographs taken by other people at other ancient sites as well, although they were not visible to the naked eye.

The other strange light experience at the Merry Maidens occurred in the Autumn of 2000 when photographer Serena Wadham observed an anomalous light and shadow occurrence that she could not explain. The sun was low in the sky before setting and the stones in the circle were casting shadows towards the north. However, as she looked at two stones in the south-west quadrant of the circle, Serena noticed that their shadows were inexplicably pointing in different directions. She had her camera with her and took a photo, reproduced below.

Opposite shadows at the Merry Maidens

There seems to be no obvious explanation for this: the stones were next to each other on the same slope of ground, so their shadows should have been pointing in the same direction.

To return to the BOLs photographed by Rodney Blunsdon at the Merry Maidens. Another variation of this is pinpricks of light that have been seen at two sites at least – Chûn Quoit [SW4023 3396] and Boleigh Fogou [SW4370 2520]. Accounts of these were first published in Paul Devereux's book *Places of Power* in 1990.[33]

---

[33] Paul Devereux *Places of Power* [Blandford, 1990] p.154-5 & 164-5.

Firstly Chûn Quoit. In the summer of 1979, archaeologist John Barnatt and photographer Brian Larkman were in Cornwall surveying the ceremonial monuments. On July 21st they set up camp near the Quoit, and in the late evening returned to the site for another look round. They each took a turn at crawling through the gap between the side slab and the capstone and sitting alone in the interior. Much to their surprise each witnessed an inexplicable light phenomenon. When looking up at the undersurface of the capstone, periodic short bursts of multicoloured light (with colours reminiscent of a rainbow) flashed across the stone's surface in short linear bands. This happened intermittently over something like 30 minutes. They both commented to each other at the time and could find no obvious explanation for the effect. It was already dark and the Quoit is situated on a hilltop which isolates it from the surrounding landscape; there are no nearby roads or tracks that allow car headlights to have been responsible. In any event, the lights were coloured.

Something similar seems to have been observed in Boleigh Fogou by Jo May, who until recently lived in the house next to the Fogou. On June 19th 1988 Jo spent the night in the underground chamber and this is what he experienced:

"Just at the point of dawn, as light was beginning to break, I saw thin spirallic filaments swirling in front of my eyes and around the main capping lintels of the passage. At first I thought it was a retinal image (much like 'floaters' or dead cells on the eyeball). But I had never experienced such spirallic phenomena before and they seemed to be moving independently of my eye movements. They most closely resembled the whorls on fingertips, but lots of them, interlaced and moving gently. Then I saw hundreds of tiny pricks of light, like stars, again moving gently, with the occasional streak as if some of them were shooting stars. I checked that this was not some kind of subjective or self-produced effect by switching my gaze back to the emerging light at the entrance of the fogou, and then redirecting my gaze several points within the passage. The stars returned unmistakably. The whole passage appeared to be filled with what can best be described as a star soup which flowed in and around the stones. Somehow I 'knew' that what I was seeing was energy, which, although subtle, was clearly 'there'. I suspect that the ability to see it depends on certain fine tuning of perception which is probably available to anyone".

Jo here seems to be getting close to the truth of what these strange lights might be about. Paul Devereux has described them as 'earth lights' and believes that they are a form of energy that comes from the earth and manifests as light. He says: "Although geological and electromegnetic factors are likely to be involved with the production of the lights, the exact mechanism of their manifestation is not yet understood, and the energy involved is exotic. It is either an unfamiliar form of electromagnetism or some as yet unidentified energy altogether. It seems to flicker in and out, as it were, on the very edge of physical manifestation, and may have revolutionary properties. It may, for example, be related to consciousness itself".[34]

That there is a link between strange lights and consciousness is evidenced from some other peculiar experiences that some people have had, usually reported as UFOs (unidentified flying objects) that appear to interact with the observers in some ways. Although UFOs are not necessarily connected with ancient sites, there have been some sightings in Cornwall at or near these places. An intriguing sighting was witnessed by myself and one other person on the ancient holy hilltop (with tumuli) of Sancreed Beacon [SW4141 2949] in the early 1990s. It was the night of the full moon and we had gone there to celebrate this. We were just setting up when we noticed to the north of us a pattern of 4 lights in the sky, making a parallelogram shape. The lights were much too high off the ground to have been distant house lights, and they were clearly not an aircraft as they remained stationary. A helicopter at night would have made some noise, and yet there was none. We were quite 'spooked' by the sighting, as it felt as if the lights were watching us and waiting for something. We decided to create a circle of protection around us, and as we began to do this, the four lights dipped up and down, as if acknowledging us, and then disappeared! It was a most inexplicable and strange event!

Strange lights and energy are somehow linked in a way that we do not fully understand, and it may well be that, as we have already seen, because the ancient sites were built on places of strong and anomalous energy, then we should expect to see strange lights coming from these places from time to time. Our ancestors who built these sites may also have seen strange lights. We do know that they were very interested in what was happening in the skies, as the next chapter shows.

---

[34] Paul Devereux *Places of Power* [Blandford, 1990] p.67-8

Chapter 7   From the Stones to the Stars
Astronomical alignments to the sun & moon

It is well documented by archaeologists that many ancient sites were constructed so as to have alignments to the rising and setting of both the sun and moon: in fact there is a whole branch of archaeology devoted to the subject called archaeo-astronomy. Professor Alexander Thom was the original exponent of this science, and his work has been continued by Clive Ruggles and others.[35] Some of the most well known sites that have astronomical alignments in Britain and Ireland are Newgrange (Ireland) with a midwinter solstice sunrise, Maes Howe (Scotland) with a midwinter solstice sunset, and Stonehenge with a midsummer solstice sunrise. But there are many hundreds more sites, less well known that have been identified as being deliberately aligned, and Cornwall is no exception.

One of the first people to investigate this in Cornwall was the early 20th century astronomer royal Sir Norman Lockyer,[36] and although some of his suggestions have been shown not to stand up to our more accurate measurements, nevertheless he laid the foundation for the work in Cornwall. In the 1960s John Michell took a fresh look at his work, and added in some suggestions of his own. With the advent of the Cornish Earth Mysteries Group in the 1990s, many more observations were made and suggestions added, so that there is now quite a considerable amount of information available.

One of the first sites identified was Tregeseal Stone Circle [SW3866 3238] , where Lockyer calculated 6 astronomical alignments. One that has been held up to scrutiny is the alignment to Boswens menhir [SW4001 3289], the tip of which is just visible on the horizon. Lockyer suggested that it marked the May Day (Beltane) sunrise, although when the CEMG checked it out in 1991, the sun rose 1° south of the actual menhir. Even allowing for the difference in the sun's rising position in the Neolithic/Bronze Age (which is only about half the sun's width when viewed from the earth), it would not have risen above the

---

[35] See for example, Clive Ruggles *Astronomy in Prehistoric Britain & Ireland* [Yale UP, 1999]
[36] Sir Norman Lockyer *Stonehenge and other British Monuments astronomically considered* [1909]

standing stone. However, it may be that the sunrise over the stone was designed to be seen not from the Tregeseal circle, but from the now-lost Soldiers Croft circle nearby [approx.SW3855 3271] from where it would have risen between 2600-1600 BCE, approximately the time when the circles would have been built. Also, the sun may have risen on the extension of the alignment to West Lanyon Quoit on the 8th May 2100 BCE (Prof.. Thom's suggestion for the date of Old Beltane), depending on the relative heights of Boswens menhir and the horizon.

One new alignment that I spotted in 1986 was from nearby Chûn Quoit [SW4023 3396]. From the Quoit the dramatic shape of Carn Kenidjack, a natural rock outcrop, is visible on the horizon to the south-west. At the midwinter solstice sunset, the sun sinks down perfectly into a distinctive sun-sized notch in the rocks. It is a beautiful piece of megalithic magic and theatre, and helps to explain why the Quoit was placed exactly where it was. Although the CEMG have visited the site every year since there, the conditions have never been good enough to see the phenomenon! However, as the climate was much better in the Neolithic, those who built the site there would have stood a much better chance of viewing it every year.

Midwinter sunset alignment from Chûn Quoit to Carn Kenidjack

Another midwinter solstice sunset alignment can be found at Bosiliack Barrow on the West Penwith moors [SW4311 3422]. Although this reconstructed barrow now lacks its covering mound, it originally would have been a kind of mini-Newgrange, and its entrance passage has the same alignment as at Newgrange, whereby the sun would have entered and shone down into the interior on the shortest day.

Bosiliack Barrow

Nearby to Bosiliack Barrow is the newly-discovered Bosiliack menhir [SW4369 3423] that lines up with nearby Carfury menhir [SW4400 3400] in a SE-NW direction (Winter solstice sunrise and Summer solstice sunset in opposite directions). At Carfury menhir itself, there is a possible midsummer solstice sunrise over Mulfra Quoit, visible on the horizon, and a midwinter solstice sunrise alignment over the tip of the Lizard peninsula, which is also visible from the site on a clear day. Distinctive marks, notches, hills and land shapes were obviously thought of as being significant to the megalithic builders. They may have had a very different concept of the Land, seeing it as the body of the Earth Mother, whom they celebrated and worshipped for her bounteousness in providing them with the means of sustenance.

This can be seen in many places. In Ireland and Scotland, distinctive breast-shaped hills like the Paps of Anu and the Paps of Jura (breasts of the Mother Goddess) were noted, and standing stones and circles placed in relationship to these sites. In West Penwith, two distinctive breast-shaped hills Chapel Carn Brea and Bartinney also seem to have been viewed in the same way. From the Merry Maidens stone circle [SW4327 2451] they are particularly noticeable: they lie in a north-westerly direction, so may have marked the midsummer solstice sunset.

Something similar was discovered by the CEMG on a visit to Trendrine Hill burial chamber [SW4785 3875] during a visit in July 1997. From the barrow a beautiful breast-shaped hill Trevalgan Hill was directly visible, facing a NE direction, that of the midsummer solstice sunrise, so that the positing of the barrow became apparent. In addition, a local woman mentioned that the hill was known colloquially as Buttermilk Hill, which is probably a vernacular memory of its nurturing Earth Mother aspect. The rising sun at the midsummer, coming up over the breast-shaped hill and entering the chamber, must have been seen as a powerful connection of the world of the living and rebirth with the world of the dead and the ancestors.

Trevalgan (Buttermilk) Hill seen from Trendrine Hill burial chamber

In the low-lying plain below Trendrine Hill lies another notable site. The remains of the Zennor stone row ends at a large (8½ft) standing stone, now used as a gatepost, the top of which formed a perfectly-shaped alignment with the top of Sperris Hill above. The angle is 112½°, which marks the Imbolc (Feb 1st) or Samhain (Nov 1st) sunrise over the hill, or from the hill the Beltane (May

1st) or Lammas (Aug 1st) sunset over the stone and the sea. Most alignments are solar, marking the solstices (Midsummer or midwinter) or the equinoxes (spring or autumn): the cross-quarter days are much rarer, so we cannot be certain that this alignment is deliberate. Nevertheless it is a dramatic sight.

Zennor stone row gatepost stone with Sperris Hill above

There are another possible couple of Samhain/Imbolc sunset alignments at stone circles in West Penwith. At Boscawen-ûn circle [SW4122 2736], when standing on the opposite side of the circle from the centre and quartz stones, an observer would see the sun set directly between the two stones at Imbolc (Feb 1st) and Samhain (Nov 1st). The bevelling of the quartz stone and centre stone seem to reinforce this interpretation. If this alignment is followed it continues to a fallen menhir at Chyangwens [SW4182 2707], the Trelew menhir [SW4217 2693], and the Toldavas stone [SW4266 2671], ending at the Castallack stone [SW4540 2545]. And at the Merry Maidens circle [SW4327 2451] the sun would have set at a similar time over the now vanished Boleigh circle and a tumulus, or alternatively, the Circle could have been viewed from these sites at the Beltane or Lammas sunrise. With all these sites and stones in place, the sunrises and sunsets must have made the land seem an enchanted place to the megalithic builders.

Finally, with the solstice alignments in West Penwith, there are a few others of interest. At Treen Common stone circle [SW4446 3666] the rising sun at midsummer would have come up through a distinctive V-shaped notch on the ridge above Zennor Hill. At Nine Maidens Boskednan circle [SW4343 3512] a now-destroyed outlying standing stone would have marked the midsummer sunrise. And from Boscawen-ûn circle [SW4122 2736] the centre stone aligned with a standing stone in the hedge [SW4147 2770] and the Blind Fiddler menhir [SW4252 2818] marks the midsummer solstice sunrise. In fact the first rays of the midsummer sun strike the base of the centre stone at the Circle, revealing two axe heads carved on the stone, visible only at this magical moment of the year. These are just some of the alignments that have been noticed by various people, which can be still viewed and checked out today, thousands of years after they were first constructed to connect with the power of the rising sun..

Moving forward in time by a couple of thousand years, we come to the Celtic Iron Age (800 BCE- 500 CE approx.) when the fogous were constructed in Cornwall. It has been shown[37] that these underground curving chambers were constructed with their northerly ends oriented to face the rising sun at the midsummer solstice, so that the first rays of light might have entered the fogou. We can imagine the people crawling down the creep passage into the fogou, and there waiting in the dark, perhaps meditating, drumming and chanting, for the first rays of light to enter the fogou, bringing the rebirth of the sun god/dess. It must have been a very powerful initiatory experience. Two fogous only do not conform to this orientation: Pendeen [SW3837 3553] and Lower Boscaswell [SW3767 3484], and in both these cases the fogou is oriented to the NW, and the setting midsummer sun. At one of the fogous, Carn Euny [SW4024 2885], there is a circular Beehive Hut attached, that preceded the fogou: it too had its entrance oriented, in this case to the rising midwinter sun. These fogous are the grand-children of the Neolithic burial bounds like Newgrange and Bosiliack Barrow, with similar ideas still at work.

Sometimes it is not just the sunrise itself that works the magic, but the interplay of light and shadow, as witnessed by Kenny May one midsummer sunrise at Carn Brea hillfort near Redruth [SW6860 4059]:[38]

---

[37] Ian Cook *Mother and Sun* [Mên-an-Tol Studio, 1993]
[38] Kenny May *Long Shadows of the Solstice Sun* [Meyn Mamvro no.27 p.3]

"I went to a spot on the south side of the hillfort where there is a 15ft standing stone and waited there to see the sun rise. I leant on the stone, and soon the sun rose over the horizon and the sky lit up. After about ½hr as the sun gained height, I noticed a shadow creeping towards me and it eventually went right up to the stone. I followed the shadow back to its source and saw a tip of a small granite stone peeping over the fern. Pushing the fern around it revealed a small standing stone some 3ft high and nicely shaped. I went back to the larger standing stone to see a shadow coming off this stone, and watched in amazement as it travelled across the ground straight to a gateway entrance, just off the line from the larger stone. On the gateway entrance it had jam stones in place going in towards the main gate post. The shadow lined up with the first stone and then moved one by one across the stones. As the sun became higher it moved off the stones and faded and disappeared into the fern, but I had been privileged to see the magic of a midsummer sunrise shadow path across the stones".

Moving up to Bodmin Moor, it seems that many of these stone circles were also oriented to the sun. In fact, the whole of Bodmin Moor seems to be like a great calendar of the wheel of the year. Starting at Beltane (early May), the sun would have risen out of a prominent notch in the holy hilltop of Rough Tor, when viewed from Stannon Circle [SX1257 8010] on the Moor.

Stannon Circle facing the notch on Rough Tor

At the Summer Solstice (June 21st-23rd) from Craddock Moor stone circle (SX2486 7183 – now ruined) the midsummer sun would have risen over Stowe's Hill, and from Leaze circle [SX1367 7729] it would have risen over Garrow Tor. Lammas (early August) would have had the same alignment as at Beltane, and at the Autumn Equinox (Sept 21st-23rd) several circles had east-west alignments (although not generally intervisible), such as the equinox sunrise seen over Brown Willy from an outlier to Fernacre Circle [SX1448 7998], and over Kilmar Tor from Goodaver Circle [SX2087 7515], the view now obscured by plantations. The equinox sunset could have been seen over Brown Willy when viewed from Leskernick North circle [SX1859 7970].

At Samhain (early Nov), the rising sun could be seen over Stowe's Hill when viewed from Goodaver Circle [SX2087 7515], and at the Winter Solstice (Dec 21st-23rd) observers at the Hurlers Circles [SX2580 7132] would have seen the sun rise sequentially over 13 barrows on Caradon Hill from Samhain onwards to the Winter Solstice, and then back again to Imbolc (early Feb). There was also a winter solstice sunset alignment over Trevarrick Tor when viewed from the now-ruined Craddock Moor Circle [SX2486 7183]. Finally, the alignments at Imbolc (early Feb) would have been the same as at Samhain, to complete the whole calendrical wheel of the year on the Moor.

There may also have been other alignments at other places. Archaeologists Peter Herring and Tony Blackman discovered a 'pseudo-quoit' or 'propped stone' (a flat stone resting on a boulder, propped up with smaller stones) on Leskernick Hill [SX1827 8019], a Neolithic and Bronze Age sacred landscape. They noticed that the midsummer sun was setting directly behind this stone, when viewed from a long low grassy mound about a mile away to the SW [SX1903 7955], which may have been constructed for the purpose. When they ran the calculations, they found that the sun would have set precisely over the distinctive stone in 3700 BCE. Also on Leskernick Hill, when the CEMG went there with archaeologist Henry Broughton in 1999, they discovered that the entrance of one of the huts ('the shaman's hut') was perfectly aligned to the top of a nearby rounded hill at the solstice sunrise. The more we discover about these places, the more that these alignments and orientations become apparent.

The final solar alignment is at the quartzite circle of Duloe in East Cornwall [SX2359 5830] which has a midwinter sunset line towards a very clear notch the other side of the valley, and also a possible equinoxical line.

Leskernick 'pseudo-quoit' marking the Midsummer sunset in 3700 BCE

Finally, in this chapter, we take a brief look at the moon and stars. Lunar alignments are much more difficult to calculate than solar ones, as the moon describes a different arc in the sky each night and takes 18.64 years to return to its original position, and 19 years for the sun and moon to occupy their same relative places in the sky. This may be why the number 19 was so important to the megalithic builders (all stone circles in West Penwith have 19 stones). Two interesting calculations of the moon have been made however. At the Mên-an-Tol holed stone (Circle) in West Penwith, it has been calculated[39] that from the centre of the circle, the northern major standstill moonrise (that only occurs every 18.64 years) would have been observed through the holed stone (if the stone was at right angles to its current position, which archaeologists believe it to have been). The moon rising at her lowest over the hills would have been framed perfectly by the holed stone, a very magical sight.

Secondly, near the Merry Maidens stone circle is a line of holed stones (some now broken or missing) running from SX4277 2431 to SX4365 2489, which have been calculated to have an azimuth also close to the northern midwinter moonrise. These holed stones could have been a powerful vehicle for the megalithic builders to have watched the moonrise every 18-19 years.

---

[39] Andy Norfolk *The Mên-an-Tol Circle Observatory* [Meyn Mamvro, no.29 p5-7]

Finally, we stay with the Merry Maidens for a curiosity originally suggested by Lockyer, whom we met a the beginning of this chapter. He believed that an observer standing at Gûn Rith standing stone [SW4294 2446], near to the circle in 1960 BCE at the end of April would have seen the Pleiades star system rising over the Circle. The Pleiades star system, also known as the Seven Sisters, was observed by many cultures, and seems to have had a great significance for many peoples. Recently, a Bronze Age disc was discovered in East Germany, depicting the sun, moon and Pleiades star system. Its observation here at the Merry Maidens at the end of April may have been to give advance warning to the megalithic builders that Beltane (May Day) was about to come, one of the great festivals in the Wheel of the Year.

Adding to this, Alan Bleakley[40] discovered that if you extend the line from the Gûn Rith menhir to the Merry Maidens circle it continues out through the entrance/exit of the circle and on to a standing stone in the corner of a hedge [SW4343 2452], through the lost Tregurmow stone circle [SW4375 2455] and finishes at a tiny place called Borah whose name means 'the place of the witch'! Bleakley points out that Goon Rith is Cornish for 'Red Downs', perhaps a reference to the setting sun in the west, and the line splits the circle into two crescents, one to the north and one to the south like two moons. A magical image to finish this look at some very amazing alignments at the stones.

Merry Maidens stone circle seen from the Gûn Rith line

---

[40] Alan Bleakley – *The Ley Hunter* no.93

Chapter 8   Where The Spirits Walk
Ghost roads & Mythic pathways

GHOST ROADS

Many sightings of ghosts and otherworldly spirits in Cornwall are very site-specific; that is, they are recorded and seen to traverse along particular routes and pathways. These ghost sightings may be some kind of psychic imprint on the landscape. Theories as to their origin include: a re-play of some past event that has left its mark on the land which recurs in certain circumstances; an archetypal image that resides in the collective unconscious, its manifestation being triggered by some altered state of consciousness on the part of the observer; or the physical manifestation of an 'energy line' of some kind running across the land – what is manifested depending on the predisposition of the observer. The answer may lie in some combination of all these theories, in a way that we do not fully understand. The following examples all come from Cornwall, and all seem to be related to a particular place in the landscape.

Firstly, hoof beats which are associated with specific old straight tracks. Jack Benny of Ventongimps near Perranporth was working in a meadow one afternoon in early summer when he heard the sound of a horse's hoof beats galloping along what is locally known as the Church Road. The hoofbeats stopped suddenly and there was no sign of any animal. Similarly, at Jamaica Inn on the old coach road that ran from Launceston to Bodmin, midnight hoofbeats have been heard, and the figure of a man on a horseback has been seen outside the Inn. Another coaching Inn that has the same sighting is the Molesworth Arms at Wadebridge. At Tregeseal farmhouse near St.Just, Chyoone farmhouse has also been the scene of phantom hoofbeats and the rumble of an unseen coach. The track of the phantom coach and horses follows an old turnpike road. And a phantom coach and horses is said to drive through Penryn just before Christmas (the old Winter Solstice).

Ghostly sightings on old tracks and roads include the following: Donald Holder and his wife Sheila were driving from Bodmin to Fowey late one evening, and just before Fowey Cross, Donald braked violently to avoid a figure on the road coming from Fowey. The figure just vanished. The publisher

Michael Williams[41] was driving along the Bodmin-Camelford road when he saw a cyclist coming in the opposite direction. The cyclist, who was wearing clothes from an earlier period, also disappeared. Another woman on a bicycle who disappeared was seen by Mary King who was taking her dog for a walk up a steep hill on the Tehidy road. A blacksmith who lived at the ancient Castle Dore [SX1030 5480] near Fowey in the early part of the 20th century saw the ghost of Squire Kendall (who had died 20 years before) walking along the road to Lostwithiel.

Castle Dore, near Fowey

One of the most interesting cases is of the faceless monk-like ghost (only about 3½ft tall) who has appeared to several people in Little Petherick on a stretch of old road that was part of the old Priest's Path (Saints Way) that stretched from Padstow to Bodmin. Alan Sandry saw it on five separate occasions.

Related to this are the sightings of ghostly figures that appear to be travelling old paths that have been superceded by modern roads. The ghost of a woman called Dorothy Dinglet has been seen walking across a field near Launceston called Higher Brown Quartils, and the path where the ghost walked was known as Dorothy Dinglet's path. The ghost of William Penvoun, the vicar of Poundstock, who was murdered on St.John's Day 1357 (Midsummer

---

[41] see Michael Williams *Supernatural in Cornwall* [Bossiney Books, 1979]

Solstice) has been seen walking down the path to the church from the top churchyard gate. In addition, at nearby Penfound Manor the ghost of Kate Penfound is supposed to appear at the hour of midnight each 26th April (close to Beltane). There is a legend of a tunnel or semi-underground passage that once linked Penfound Manor with Poundstock Church, a mile and a quarter away, and legends of underground passages are often folk memories of ancient ghost paths or ley lines.

In this category, I have a sighting of my own. The incident took place some time between 1976-1979 when a friend and myself were driving late one evening on the lower road from Gunnislake to Calstock, where my late father then lived. It is a quiet road and there was no other traffic. At some point along the road, both my friend and I saw ahead of us in the car headlights a line of men crossing the road. This was unusual on two counts: one, they had on their heads old-fashioned miners' helmets with candles as lights, and two, they seemed to cross the road and 'disappear' into the wall beside the road. They were crossing in an east to west direction. I remember saying to my friend 'What was that?' and she said something about it being very strange. As I drove past, I looked in my rearview mirror but saw nothing behind me. The area we were driving through is littered with tin and copper mines dating from the 18th and 19th centuries. After that, I mentioned it to a few people over the years, but it was not until some years later that I received a startling confirmation of my sighting. My father used to send me regularly copies of the weekly local paper *The East Cornwall Times.* One day when I received it I was amazed to see a headline that a Gunnislake woman had seen the ghosts of miners walking across a road. As far as I recall, this was the same road where I had seen my 'vision'. The following week two other local women wrote to the paper to say that they too had witnessed the same sighting. The miners may have been following an old trackway which is not now there.

There are also three very interesting animal sightings that hint of the geomythic significance of ancient paths. Firstly, a ghostly white hare is reputed to run from Talland to Looe and there vanish at the door of the Jolly Sailor Inn. She is supposed to be the spirit of a girl who killed herself, and the whole legend may hark back to a pre-Christian spirit path, hares being traditionally an animal sacred to the Goddess. The legend of Boleigh fogou near Lamorna in West Penwith [SW4370 2520] tells of Squire Lovell who is chasing a hare across the land who goes down into the fogou. Squire Lovell follows it and when he gets in there, he discovers a coven of witches doing a ritual.

Secondly, at the old Dog and Dragon restaurant at Porthtown, a spectral dog has been seen, mostly on May Day (Beltane). There is an old legend here that a dragon used to haunt the neighbourhood until seen off one May Eve by a dog. Again, we have a pre-Christian legend, dragons originally representing the telluric currents of the earth. Finally, at the old ruined chapel that lies hidden near Tregerthen [SW4670 3925] between Zennor and Wicca on the old Zennor churchway or coffin path, an eerie fox-like creature was seen on top of the walls one afternoon by author Mary Williams. Craig Weatherhill has commented: "It is this stretch of path which most strongly retains a sense of otherworldliness, which is instantly felt by anyone walking its route."[42] There is another hare connection here too: in Trewey, next to Zennor, a witch transformed herself into a hare in order to get food from St.Ives, five miles away, for her husband's dinner; the route she took was the same as the churchway.

Tregerthen Chapel on the old Zennor churchway path

All this leads us in the realm of myth and legend, which is where we turn next for a look at the related topic of mythic pathways.

---

[42] Craig Weatherhill *The Ley Hunter* no.118

MYTHIC PATHWAYS

Church paths abound throughout Cornwall: they were medieval trackways that led from farmsteads through parishes to the nearby Church. People would walk them regularly to and from the Church, and many have ancient Celtic crosses standing on them. They were also the route whereby the dead were carried in walking funerals from the farm to the church, so they also became known as 'death roads' or 'corpse ways'. Because the farms were often built on much earlier Celtic and Iron Age settlements, and because the Churches often stand on places that were prehistoric sacred spots (such as St.Eval Church which stands on a pre-Christian round and incorporates some megalithic standing stones in its churchyard wall), these routes may be much older than the medieval period. Some of them have ancient legends linked to them, which we may call mythic routes, for the power of old Celtic myths are often directly related to the landscape.

One such mythic pathway, already mentioned (above) is the Zennor Churchway Path in West Penwith. It runs from St.Ives to Zennor, and then continues westwards in parts towards Morvah. It is marked with many cross sites, but also with earlier standing stones (or sites of them), and the path passes three parish churches, St.Ives, Zennor and Morvah, but avoids each one.

Witch's Rock near Zennor

57

At two places along the route, Burn Downs near Tregarthen (site of the Chapel mentioned above), and at the Witch's Rock or Giant's Rock near Zennor [SW4540 3835], all the witches in West Penwith were reputed to meet on Midsummer Eve. There are many associations of witchcraft and other-worldliness linked to this pathway, including a witch transforming herself into a hare (mentioned above) and running along the path.

Another such mythic pathway, first identified by Paul Devereux[43] and visited by CEMG in June 1998 is that which runs down the Porthcurno Valley to St.Levan Church. The CEMG visited Bodellan farmhouse [SW3840 2315], where it has been claimed that the grave of St.Levan has been discovered in a mound by dowsing. From here the path goes on down the road and across fields to the hamlet of Rospletha, where on the path there is a old cross [SW3820 2222]. It then changes direction to goes directly into the back of St.Levan Churchyard, where there is a huge boulder dolmen with a split down the centre, and an old legend, variously attributed to St.Levan or to Merlin, that says if a packhorse ever passes through the crack it will be the end of the world.

CEMG at St.Levan's Stone

The path can in fact be traced even further down from the Church to a holy well and the remains of a small chapel on the cliffside below [SW3811 2198].

---

[43] Craig Weatherhill & Paul Devereux *Myths and Legends of Cornwall* [Sigma, 1994] p.154

The mythic significance of this line is that the old legends say that St.Levan himself followed this path regularly from Bodellan to his chapel, below which he used to fish. One Sunday a woman called Johanna rebuked him for going fishing on the Sunday, and it is said that since then no girl in the Parish has ever been called Johanna. It was said that on the path where St.Levan walked "the grass grows greener than in any other part of the fields through which the footpath passes". Clearly, a very ancient and beneficent mythic path.

Other possible mythic pathways include the route running from St.Keverne on the Lizard to St.Just in West Penwith. Here the Celtic saint St.Keverne lived, and one day he was visited by his brother St.Just who stole a rare cup off him. St.Just ran back across the land, via Breage, with St.Keverne in hot pursuit, throwing great stones after him. Three of these fell to the ground beside the road between Breage and Germoe, where they remained until broken up at the turn of the 20th century.

The throwing of rocks by the saints, or alternatively the giants, in Cornish legend, is perhaps a memory of the geomantic significance of the Land. The giants of Trencrom Hill [SW5180 3618] used to play bowls with the great boulders lying around, and one of these, the Bowl Rock [SW5189 3670] still remains in a garden at the bottom of the hill. The chief giant of the Hill Trebcromm was a friend of the giant of St.Michael's Mount, Cormoran. They used to throw hammers to each other, across the intervening land, which again may be the memory of a geomantic and geomythic pathway. There is a direct ley alignment between the church spire of St.Ives on the north coast, Trencrom Hill [SW5180 3615] in the centre and St.Michael's Mount [SW5145 2985] on the south coast. One day one of the hammers hit Cormelian, wife of Cormoran, on the head killing her outright. She was buried beneath Chapel Rock, a solitary greenstone rock that had been dropped there by Cormelian herself. It marks the beginning of the causeway to the Mount, and is perhaps a memory of a sacred passageway across to the Mount.

Another giant wont to throw things was Bolster, who could stand with one foot on St.Agnes Beacon [SW7090 5060] and the other on Carn Brea [SW6850 4060] – the two hills are in fact 6 miles apart! Another version of the legend says that he and the giant of Carn Brea would throw rocks at each other. The same legend is attached to the giant of Warbstow Bury hill fort [SX2020 9080] who was killed by a tool thrown at him by the giant of Launceston Castle.

St.Michael's Mount and the Greenstone Rock marking the causeway route

The ubiquitousness of this legend all over Cornwall is an indication of its important and powerful antecedence. It may be a distant memory of the megalithic builders who first shaped and changed the Land, and the powerful energy lines and spirit paths that linked together the ancient sites and the holy hilltops. Where the old saints and giants and witches walked or ran or threw stones are the mythic pathways across the land, where the stories and songs of our ancestors would have been told and sung, the Cornish equivalent of the Aboriginal song lines.

Chapter 9   Lost in the Mists of Time
Piskey-led with the Fairy folk

"A man named Bottrell who lived near St.Teath was piskey-led at West Down, and when he turned his pockets inside out he heard the piskies going away laughing. Sometimes it is necessary to turn your coat inside out. A Zennor man said that to do the same thing with your socks or stockings is as good."[44]

Legends of the piskies or little-folk abound in Cornwall, and a very specific aspect of this is the notion of being piskey-led. To be piskey-led is to be led astray, to loose your way or your path, because the piskey-folk have somehow altered the familiar terrain, or in some mysterious ways, the traveller's perception of it. This has relevance to Earth Mysteries studies of haunted highways, and/or paths of the dead running across the land, either visibly or invisibly.

Jeremy Hart has suggested[45] that piskey-leading may be the development of three distinct types of tale: the mocking guide, the aimless wandering, and the deluded confinement. However, he also explores the possibility that it may be a geophysical state: "It is tempting to see it as a product of certain localised physical energies, which will act on anyone coming within their field of force and lead to an altered state in which the core phenomenon, simple disorientation, is more or less elaborated according to cultural variables". In other words, the same anomalous geomantic energies at certain 'hotspots' in the land that can give rise to other visionary experiences (such as UFOs, ghosts, etc) can also lead to the experience of being piskey-led, when the belief in that phenomenon is widely accepted in the society, as it was in Cornwall right up until the 19th century.

If this theory has any credence, we should expect to find accounts of being piskey-led set in very specific parts of the landscape, and not in some vague no-man's land. Is this in fact what we find or not? Let's examine the evidence in Cornwall

---

[44] J.Evans-Wenz *Fairy Faith in Celtic Countries* [OUP, 1911] p.183
[45] Jeremy Hart *Pixie Leading* [Third Stone, no.20 Spring 1995]

One of the best-known 'piskey-led' cases concerns one Uter Boscence who was led astray as he was returning from St.Just to Sancreed one evening after a hurling match.[46] When he got to the field at Bosence, called Park-an-Chapel (the site of an old Celtic chapel) a cloud of fog rose from the moors, so thick that he could scarcely see a yard in front of him. He walked towards where he knew there was an opening in the field, but when he got there no opening was to be found. He tried to climb over the hedge, but the more he climbed the higher the hedge became. At the ruins of the old chapel, he saw "the most frightful sprights and spriggans one ever beheld" and encountered a demonic being that sent him "rolling down the field, tossed over the hedge, pished through the brambles and furze, pitched over the bogs, and whirled away like dust before the wind." The significance of this story is not only the place where it occured (site of an old Celtic chapel) but also the time, it being midsummer night, the time of the old pagan festival, when bonfires were still lit on the hilltops. So we have here a doubly potent 'between the worlds of time and space' setting for the experience to occur.

Places such as the old Celtic chapel of Bosence were often thought to be special places where one could encounter the Otherworld. In the story given above, the collector Bottrell says: "The ugliest of sprights and spriggans, with other strange apparitions, such as unearthly lights, were often seen hovering around the ruins of the old chapel." Another collector, Hunt tells[47] how an old man who got piskey-led in the area would often shelter at Caer Bran (Iron Age hillfort) "for everyone knew that anywhere within the Rings on Brane Hill, the same as for Bartinney, nothing evil that wanders the earth by night could harm them".

Another such place was "the green outside the gate at the end of Tresidder Lane" near St.Levan, a very specific location for another tale of piskey-leading. The green may have originally been a gathering place in ancient times: certainly some open spaces like this became known as special places. Hunt says that this green was a favourite place with the Small Folk to hold their fairs. A Mr. Trezillian returning late one night from Penzance saw them and went to investigate. They were all over him like a swarm of bees, his horse ran off and he didn't know what to do "till by good luck he thought of what he had often heard, so he turned his glove inside out, threw it amongst the Small Folk,

---

[46] William Bottrell *Hearthside Stories of West Cornwall* [Vol 1,. 1870] p.59-61
[47] Robert Hunt *Popular Romances of the West of England* [Vol 1, 1871] p.119

and ere the glove reached the ground they were all gone." He now had to find his horse, and the Small Folk, still determined to lead him astray, bewildered him. He was piskie-led, and he could not find out where he was until broad daylight. Then he saw he was only a hundred yards from the place at where he had left his horse.[48]

Mr Trezillian was returning from Penzance, and this illustrates the tendency of people to be piskey-led when they are going along everyday routes rather than being 'lost on the moors'. For example, an old man named Glasson was piskey-led one bright moonlit night: "He was returning to Ludgvan from Gulval, but no matter which path he took it led him back to where he had started. At last he turned his coat inside out, the only way to break the spell, and reached Ludgvan without further trouble."[49]

Another tale which has great geomythic significance is the legend of Pee Tregeer, who was able to see a fairy at Penzance market due to her illicit use of a "greenish ointment". The tale[50] is very specific about the route she took back from Penzance to Pendeen: "She didn't return by way of Polteggan Bottom and Boswednan, though it's the nearest .... she took her course through Castle Horneck fields". After three or four miles she begins to enter what we would call a state of altered consciousness "being so distracted she couldn't tell whether she was going up hill or down dale half the way". She has a vision of man on a horseback which metamorphoses into a cross, meets a piskey thresher at Boslow, and finally on the Gump near Carn Kenidjack is piskey-led, encountering amongst other things little folk with a goblet in the shape of a poppy capsule. Weatherhill and Devereux[51] suggest that this is an opium reference, and this would certainly fit with the notion of the event occuring in a state of altered consciousness.

---

[48] Robert Hunt *Popular Romances of the West of England* [Vol.3, 1871] p.181
[49] Tony Deane & Tony Shaw *The Folklore of Cornwall* [Batsford, 1975] p.90
[50] William Bottrell *Hearthside Stories of West Cornwall* [Vol 2, 1873] p.154-66
[51] Craig Weatherhill & Paul Devereux *Myths & Legends of Cornwall* [Sigma, 1994] p.161

The Gump near Carn Kenidjack with Tregeseal Circle in foreground

They also make the point that the route An Pee takes is a specific geomythic path across the landscape. It is also an event, like the Uter Bosence one, that occurs at a time outside of time, namely the eve of Halloween (the old Celtic festival of Samhain). In addition, to further reinforce the point, she has a vision on the Gump of the Little People celebrating Beltane with maypole and garlands. So An Pee has been transported in time by exactly half-a-year to the mirror-image pagan Celtic beginning of Summer festival. The tale thus contains all the elements that link it to a time and space before and beyond the present: a visionary experience that occurs by taking narcotics, in which the veil between the worlds disappears, and An Pee moves freely between this world and the Otherworld. She gains entry into this Otherworld by taking a specific mythic route across the land.

One tale[52] that illustrates the protagonist moving through time is that of John Sturtridge, who, when walking home to Luxulyan, meets a party of Little People at Tregarden Down. He becomes piskey-led: "The Down, well known from early experience, became like ground untrodden, and after a long trial no gate or stile was to be found". In this case, he not only becomes disoriented, but is transported many miles away to the beach at Par, where he is led to the wine

---

[52] Robert Hunt *Popular Romances of the West of England* [Vol 1, 1871] p.89

cellar of Squire Tremain. He is found the next morning, and sentenced to hang for his misdemenour, but at his execution a "little lady" appears (one of the piskey folk in disguise) and with a shout of "Ho and away to France" he is once again transported through time to effect his escape. Here we have perhaps a late memory of some ritual formula or incantation that was used by ancient peoples to 'time-travel', that is, to go on shamanic journeys to the spirit world. As we have seen, many of these piskey-led tales contain elements that hint of such earlier ritual and shamanic practices.

Another similar tale of altered consciousness comes from the Rev. Baring-Gould, writing about Parson Hawker, the Vicar of Morwenstow in 1876.[53] He tells the story of a man returning home from market and passing between dense hedges, who saw a light and heard music and singing. Looking through the hedge, he saw an elf sitting on a toadstool, holding a lantern formed from a campanula flower, from which poured a greenish-blue light. A group of fairies was dancing in a ring. The man described what he did: "I looked and listened a while, and then I got quietly hold of a great big stone and heaved it up, and I dreshed in amongst them all, and then I up on my horse and galloped away as hard as I could, and never drew rein until I came home to Morwenstow. Next day I went back to the spot, and there lay the stone, just where I had dreshed it."

Many of the elements of the 'transported in time' motif are here: the man following a prescribed route home, "between tall hedges" and thus deprived of landscape features, seeing a light, having a vision, which included the fairy with a flower that gave off an ethereal other-worldy light, and then returning to see nothing there. Janet Bord speculates[54] that the man may have come under the influence of some electro-magnetic energy which caused him to see the fairies who were really there, the lantern being the light from the power source. Or alternatively, he may have hallucinated the elf and the dancing fairies when he came under the influence of an electro-magnetic discharge.

Finally, if such journeys through space and time existed in earlier days and were still being written about in disguised form in the 19th century, have they altogether disappeared in our 'age of reason'? Katherine Briggs suggests

---

[53] S.Baring Gould *The Vicar of Morwenstow* [1876] p.164
[54] Janet Bord *Fairies: Real Encounters with Little People* [Michael O'Mara Books, 1997] p.141

not. She recounts[55] a story recorded in 1961 which tells of a woman who went to a house in Cornwall to do some secretarial work. When the farm came into sight she walked in and asked if she were on the right track to the Manor. She was given careful directions, but couldn't find the second white gate to go through. "I had a most creepy feeling" she said. "I went all along the hedge but there was only one gate. Then somebody came up the bridle track whistling, and the thick mist cleared and there was no hedge. It was one of the farm lads sent after me who knew what to do. 'Here's your white gate, Miss' he said, and sure enough, there it was beside the other one".

I also have a tale from my personal experience. One night a group of us went up to the top of Bartinney Hill in West Penwith to celebrate one of the festivals. When we had finished (about midnight) we started to come down, but became totally lost and disoriented. Then one of us (who happened to be a Bard of the Cornish Gorsedd) said "We've been piskey-led. Anyone with change in their pocket turn it over". Several of us did, and immediately we found ourselves on the correct path, and made our way to the bottom of the hill, where an examination of our watches showed the time to be 4am! Were we piskey-led on that night that lay between the worlds? We should never underestimate the power of the Otherworld: it lies all around us today, as the next chapter shows.

Bartinney Hill (right) & Chapel Carn Brea (left)

---

[55] Katherine Briggs *The Fairies in Tradition and Literature* [Routledge, 1967]] p.138

Chapter 10   Journeys to the Otherworld
Stories and Dreams of the Enchanted Land

THE OTHERWORLD IN CORNISH LEGEND

Most Celtic literature and myth has the concept of an 'Otherworld': in Irish it was known as 'Aes Sidhe' and in Welsh folklore Annwfyn or Annwn. This 'Otherworld' had many other names and manifestations, including the Tir-na-nog "The Land of Youth", Tir-Innambeo "The Land of the Living", Tir Tairngire "The Land of Promise" and Tir N-aill "The Other World". It was also thought to consist of the Upperworld, the Middle World and the Underworld, and in many stories it is the place occupied by the ancestors. Often the hero goes in search of the ancient dead, as it is they who remember and preserve the traditions of older times. However, the Otherworld generally is not a place of doom and gloom. Rather than an ending of life, the Otherworld of the Celts is a gateway into another kind of life. Often this life looks very much like our everyday life, though it is transformed by its beauty and by Otherworldly creatures who inhabit it. It is in fact a "magical idealised mirror image of the human world".[56]

The creatures who inhabit this world include the dead ancestors, but also gods, spirits, supernatural creatures and strange beasts – as well as the fairy folk. The place of the Otherworld is also a place out of time – time moves at a different pace and if an ordinary mortal enters the Otherworld, he or she does not grow any older there. However, if she or he then returns to the everyday world, time has passed and all his or her companions have grown older.

Other common elements in the Celtic stories include the passage into the Otherworld, which is often into a burial mound or 'fairy mound', or across or under water. The time for entering the Otherworld is often at the Celtic festivals, when the boundaries between the earthly and supernatural worlds is broken down and spirits and humans can move freely between the two lands. Evans-Wenz says:[57] "The Celtic Otherworld is like that hidden realm of subjectivity lying just beyond the horizon of mortal existence, which we cannot behold when we would, save with the mystic vision of the (Celtic) seer". He

---

[56] Miranda Green *Dictionary of Celtic Myth and Legend* [Thames & Hudson, 1998]
[57] W.Evans-Wenz *The fairy Faith in Celtic Countries* [1911]

points out that all Celtic nations have their mythic islands off-shore, which were often thought to be the dwelling-place of the Otherworld: in Brittany it was called Ys; in Wales it was known as Caer Arianrhod; and in Cornwall of course the lost land of Lyonesse. There was also a legend that the Isles of Scilly were the place of the dead, where souls went after death to rest. In Welsh myth "Cornwall" often becomes a metaphor for a kind of Celtic Otherworld to where Arthur chases a boar and disappears into the sea, and where Bran's men open a door to the land and come face to face with all their grief.

The Scillies: islands of the Blest or the Dead

It is however the stories recorded by both Robert Hunt and William Bottrell in the late 19th Century that perhaps furnish us with the best folkloric evidence of the concept of an Otherworld in Cornwall. One of the most powerful of these stories is one recorded by Bottrell as 'Fairy Dwelling on Selena Moor'.[58] The story concerns the disappearance of a farmer William Noy, and how, after three days, he is discovered apparently asleep on a stretch of boggy ground near Selena Moor. When he comes to, he tells a strange story of taking a short cut across the moor and getting lost in a part of the moor he had never seen before. After wandering many miles, he heard strains of music and spied lights glimmering. He then saw hundreds of Little People, amongst whom was one Grace Hutchens, who had formerly been his sweetheart until she had

---

[58] William Bottrell *Traditions & Hearthside Stories of West Cornwall* [Vol. 2, 1873]

died 3 or 4 years before. She had in fact been abducted by the Fairie Folk, all of whom were originally mortals who had lived thousands of years ago. This makes explicit the nature of the Otherworld as the dwelling place of ghosts of prehistoric people.

The Otherworld is also described by Grace Hutchens as a "beautiful garden with alleys all boarded by roses and many sweet flowers that she had never seen the light of. Apples and other tempting fruit dropped in the walks and hung overhead, bursting ripe." Significantly, the garden is also described as being surrounded by trees and water. And perhaps most significantly of all, the Fairy Folk are described as "not of our religion, but star-worshippers", perhaps a pagan belief of the Ancestors, and a memory of the solar and lunar alignments of the megalithic builders [see Ch.7]. Grace also speaks of being able to take the form of any bird she pleases, and shape-shifting was also a common Celtic motif.

The road to the Otherworld through caves and mounds, so typical of Irish and Welsh tales, may also be found in the Cornish story of the young farmer Richard Vingoe, who follows a path into an underground passage on Treville Cliffs, and, on emerging, finds himself in a "strange pleasant-looking country" that is Fairyland. Here he too meets his former lover who has been dead a few years, and in this case she leads him back to the Upper World by a shorter road through an opening in a carn. In another story, the Lost Child of St.Allen[59], a young child is taken to the Other World by being lured by some beautiful music that leads him to the centre of a dark grove. A passage appears before him as if made by some invisible being, and he finds himself on the edge of a small lake. He falls asleep, which is the prelude to crossing the liminal threshold between this world and the Otherworld. He is then taken "by a beautiful lady through palaces of the most gorgeous description". "Pillars of glass supported arches which glistened with every colour and there were hung with crystals far exceeding anything which were ever seen in the caverns of a Cornish mine". Eventually, he is restored to the everyday world. The story includes many of the elements found in the Welsh and Irish annals: the beautiful music leading to the Otherworld, the place surrounded by a lake or at the bottom of a lake, and the beautiful state of the Land itself.

---

[59] Robert Hunt *Popular Romances of the West of England* [Vol. 1, 1871]

69

Although the stories of the Cornish Otherworld are never specifically described as "the Otherworld", it is clear that this is what they are. In the story of "Cherry of Zennor"[60] for example, there are a number of important trigger words in the story to indicate to the reader that s/he is on a journey to the Otherworld. Cherry meets a "gentleman" at a *cross roads* (a magical place of transformation), and he takes her on a journey through lanes where "sweet briars and honeysuckles perfumed the air, and the reddest of ripe apples hung from the trees over the lane". The fecundity of nature where everything grows abundantly is always a hint that we are on the way to the Otherworld. Then they come to a "stream of water as clear as a crystal, which ran across the lane" where the man carries her across. Streams and rivers are usually liminal places, marking the division between this world and the Otherworld. Having crossed the stream, they arrive at a garden where everything is more intensely beautiful than anything in the everyday world. "Flowers of every dye were around her; fruits of all kinds hung above her; and the birds, sweeter of song than any she had ever heard, burst out into a chorus of rejoicing". Cherry is taken into a house which was "yet more beautiful". "Flowers of every kind grew everywhere, and the sun seemed to shine everywhere, and yet she did not see the sun". Cherry spends some time in this enchanted land, looking after the house and the Master's child, but it is no ordinary place. One room contains people who have been turned to stone, and Cherry has some ointment put on her eyes which gives her the gift of seeing the Fairy Folk. Eventually she returns to the "real world" but is forever changed by the experience.

Stories such as these seem to be predicated upon a deeply-held belief, probably dating from Celtic times if not before, that there was an Otherworld that existed in parallel to our own, and could be accessed when the veil between the worlds was thin enough. Interestingly, new scientific theories in cosmology posit the likelihood of there really being parallel universes to our own, populated by beings similar to ourselves, and yet different in some essential details. The stories also have the feel of being not dissimilar to those experienced in dreams or on psychedelic trips, and it was to explore this link between sites in the land and human consciousness that the Dragon Project set up a 'Dream Team' experiment at certain sites in Cornwall and elsewhere in the 1990s. The first results of this research have just been published.

---

[60] Ibid.

DREAMING INTO THE OTHERWORLD

There is a long history of people dreaming at sacred sites, usually for purposes of initiation, divination or healing. From Mesopotamia to Ancient Egypt and China, incubation chambers were constructed at sacred temple sites. The Hypogeum at Malta and the Dream temples at Athens and Epidauras in Greece are well known, but there were well over 300 dream temples (many dedicated to the healing god Aesculapius) throughout the Greek and Roman worlds. The Dragon Project Trust chose four sites for their experiment, one in Wales and three in Cornwall: Chûn Quoit [SW4023 3396], Carn Euny fogou [SW4024 2885] and Madron Baptistry [SW4465 3280]. At these sites volunteers went for the night to sleep and dream, accompanied by a therapeute, who would stay awake, and when the volunteers started dreaming (as evidenced by REM sleep – rapid eye movement) the therapeute would wake him or her and immediately record the dream. The purpose was to discover whether the sites had any influence on the dreams: in other words were there any similarities between all the different dreams that could be more than chance, and might be attributed to the location of the sleeper. Paul Devereux, whose idea this originally was, comments: "I wondered if there could be information at long-used special sites that could be detected by the unconscious (dreaming) mind but inaccessible to the waking intellect. We (also) wanted to find out if there were site-specific characteristics in the dreams – themes, sequences, images, motifs, symbols, even colours – that could be identified."[61]

Chûn Quoit – one of the dream incubation sites

---

[61] Paul Devereux *Dragon Dreams* [Fortean Times 178, Dec 2003] p.30-35

Some 70 volunteers dreamed at the sites, with 60 producing on-site dream reports, of which 35 also submitted home dreams as a control. Two judges, working blind and independently, evaluated each of the 206 dream reports, using the Strauch Scale which contains criteria for identifying 'bizarre' 'magical' and 'paranormal' elements. The results[62] were inconclusive, with only a slight difference between the elements identified in site dreams with those from home dreams. However, some of the dreams themselves make for interesting reading. These are a few examples from the dreams of some people at the Carn Euny fogou:-

"A sense of processing... ritual of going from one place to another (MVB)
"I dreamt that we broke into a new tomb somewhere near here" (DS)
"Stuck on the wall was a big round thing and it had a face on it...It wasn't really a human face..It had big, roundish eyes." (BH)
"Little boy with an old face, deformed face or something. It was slightly nightmare-ish" (GH)[63]

This dream extract is from a volunteer at Chûn Quoit:-

"First I dreamt that I was floating 10 feet above my body. Then I dreamt I came back to earth (with a jolt) only to be greeted by an undertaker (complete with ribboned hat and hearse" (AH)[64]

These dream snatches seem to be about going on a journey to another state of being, and connecting with another realm of experience. The AH dream is especially interesting, as it appears at the beginning to be an out-of-body experience (OOBE). AH comments on what he felt about dreaming there:

"The experience of almost ten years ago made a strong impression. Not least, it convinced me that Chûn Quoit is a place of extraordinary power, where the veil is thin and that can inspire lucid dreaming and OOBEs. I believe it is connected with spiritual growth and death (possibly ritual). I believe that Chûn Quoit is most definitely linked to shamanic practices"[65]

---

[62] see Krippner, Devereux & Fish *The use of the Strauch Scale to study dream reports from Sacred Sites in England and Wales* [Dreaming Vol 13, no.2 June 2003]
[63] from Paul Devereux *Dragon Dreams* [Fortean Times 178, Dec 2003] p.34
[64] Pers. Comm. from Andrew Hassall 21/01/04
[65] Ibid.

The lucid dreams mentioned by AH above were also a feature of other dreams at the sites. Lucid dreams are those where a person's normal consciousness switches on inside a dream while they remain asleep, so it seems as if the dream is as real as everyday experience. A high percentage of the volunteers had such lucid and semi-lucid dreams at the sites, statistically higher than the home dreams recorded. There were also many dreams with magical and paranormal themes. Krippner et.al. comment:[66] "Several site dream reports contained elements reminiscent of ancient and mythical Cornwall, for example "Jurassic rock", "a cave in the earth", "a stone tomb", "a labyrinth", "a stone circle", "a cave painting", "a hag" and "magicians", though the home dreams also contained similar elements." One site dream recorded "a round table of ancient scholars whose robes were red and emitted a special musical key". In another the dreamer reported "the entrance to a celestial palace" (shades of Richard Vingoe's journey to the Otherworld, described above): the dreamer wanted to explore beyond the gates but first she had to perform a task.

This brings us full circle back to the Otherworld experiences recorded in the earlier part of this chapter. Could it be that the very vivid and detailed Otherworld journeys taken by the protagonists in the Cornish stories were the result of lucid dreaming? And that what was dreamed was thought to have actually happened? And to take speculation one step further: could it be that lucid dreaming is really as 'real' as everyday 'reality', that it is not 'merely' a dream, but a different state of consciousness, an alternative reality, a parallel universe? If this is the case, then the Otherworld visited by William Noy, Richard Vingoe, Cherry of Zennor and others was not just a 'fairy story' but a genuine experience of visiting an alternative reality, accessed through a waking dream or sleeping experience. The Otherworld may indeed be all around us as we go through our everyday life's journey. In the final chapter, we look at some experiences of people at ancient sites in Cornwall, who have had shifts of reality that have allowed them to gain glimpses of the sites at other times and places.

---

[66] Krippner, Devereux & Fish *The use of the Strauch Scale to study dream reports from Sacred Sites in England and Wales* [Dreaming Vol 13, no.2 June 2003] p.101

Chapter 11   Opening the Veil Between the Worlds
Altered states of consciousness

Dreaming is one way of moving into an altered state of consciousness, but there are others as well. Meditation, ritual drumming, and the ingestion of locally-grown narcotic plants would all probably have been used by ancient peoples at the sites to attain mind-changing experiences, and go on 'spirit journeys' to connect with the spirits of the ancestors. Meditation was used as a means of going on spirit journeys by a group of volunteers with the CEMG in 1992-5. These 'imaging' sessions took place at Halligye fogou [SW7132 2395] and Boscawen-ûn circle [SW4122 2736], and produced some interesting results.

At the first session at Halligye fogou, about two dozen people sat in the fogou in silence in the dark, and just focussed on clearing their minds and letting images come in at random. Afterwards, they compared the results, and there were a number of common links. In particular several people experienced 'flying' sensations in which they seemed to be free of the fogou confines. This could have been the first part of a spirit journey, and it would be interesting to repeat the experiment but take longer time. At the second session, several people had images of suns with rays and of shapes and faces in the rock. These are known as entropic images, and have been recorded by native peoples from various cultures, including the aboriginal people, all over the world. It was at this session that the Group also heard the chirruping noises mentioned in Ch.5.

At Boscawen-ûn circle in July 1993, eleven people meditated and then compared images afterwards. Many images were found in common, including eyes (6), lines and grids (5), golden-yellow colours (6) and cow/bull horns (3). These were not particularly obvious or predictable images, though all are archetypal cultural symbols. Eyes are well attested at prehistoric Old European sites, and are thought to be a symbol of the Goddess. In Egypt the eye was specifically associated with Horus, and the 'Eye of Horus' is a symbol still seen widely in the Mediterranean today. Likewise, cow and bull horns were widely known in ancient Cretan societies as Goddess symbols. Lines and grids have an interesting link to earth energy patterns, and golden yellow images could be sun iconography. All in all, it was a very interesting session, that could be repeated.

Boscawen-ûn circle, location for the imaging session

Boscawen-ûn circle seems to be a powerful place for visioning, and other experiences have been recorded here. One was given by the late Jean Harris in 1996:[67]

"It was the first Sunday in May, and as we walked along the path towards Boscawen-ûn circle, the power of the stones came to meet us. This was Miriam's birthday and we had come to celebrate. We sat within the circle, backs against the stones and silently meditated. The sun was deliciously warm on our faces, the air scented with gorse blossom and the special magic of May month quickened the atmosphere.

As I drifted into the Other World, I found myself in a space-craft hovering over the site. The craft began to move silently through the air and when it came to a standstill, I looked out of a huge rectangular window and saw below the waters of Mounts Bay. The sunny day had turned to a cold, winter one; the sea was grey and empty apart from one solitary cargo ship which seemed to be in some sort of distress. The scene was bleak, silent and brooding. Within seconds, I found myself back at Boscawen-ûn and the beauty of the warm, scented day, relieved to feel the grass under my toes and the strength of the stone at my back.

---

[67] Jean Harris *Cerridwen's Cauldron* [Meyn Mamvro, no.30 p.21]

75

It wasn't until we were driving back home that the sick shock left my solar plexus.

The following November, Miriam was given the devastating news that she had advanced cancer. A few days before Christmas, we were at the house of one of our Group members for a Yuletide party. The house was high up on Paul Hill and we had all gathered on the balcony to look down at the lights in the harbour. Miriam was holding on to my arm, weak and ill from her radiotherapy treatment, and as I looked across at Mount's Bay I felt a sick shock in my solar plexus, for there, listing on its side was one solitary cargo ship. People were talking about it, how it had been widely reported in the media, this foreign ship which had dragged itself into the harbour in great distress.

Miriam died on a beautiful summer day and as I held her hand, I found myself at Boscawen-ûn with a brilliant light in the sky above me. I knew this was the light which had come to take her over to her new life. A few days later I went to Boscawen-ûn for my Farewell ritual to Miriam."

Boscawen-ûn was also the location for a psychic experience of my own. My black cat (called Sabbat of course!) had gone missing about a week earlier, after being hit by a car. I had searched everywhere for her without any success and was now giving up, thinking that she must have crawled away to die. So I went to the circle, and at the quartz stone, I sent out my spirit to her to give her a safe passage to the 'other side'. I was very fond of her, so it was an emotional experience, and I returned home feeling wiped out, so went to bed. There I slept and had a vivid dream of Sabbat, in which she was still alive in a shed of some kind, and in the dream she dragged herself back to the house, but only had enough energy to get to the side door of the house, not the door with the cat flap. I awoke, feeling quite shaken by this, but later that evening I heard a faint mew outside the house, and when I went to investigate there she was at the side door, just as in the dream. I rushed her to the vets, and though she lost her tail, she did survive. I can only think that the connection I made to her spirit, amplified by the quartz stone at Boscawen-ûn, was transmitted through the ether to her mind, and it gave her the strength to drag herself back. The power of the stone helped to open my psychic channels, which is why I had the precognitive dream when I returned home.

Other powerful sites for psychic experiences seem to be the fogous in West Cornwall. Halligye fogou has already been mentioned, and other fogou sites also seem to be particularly 'charged' for experiences of altered states of consciousness. One of the most interesting of these was the experience recounted by Jackie Sutton:[68] at Carn Euny fogou [SW4024 2885]

"My fiancé and I enjoyed a wonderful holiday in St.Just. We chose Cornwall to explore umpteen Celtic/Pagan sites, but went to the areas open-minded, not with pre-conceived ideas. One hot day we visited Carn Euny fogou. After having explored it, my boyfriend decided to cool off in the fogou itself. I myself couldn't go in: it wasn't an unpleasant feeling. I just knew I *shouldn't* go in at *that* particular time. So instead I propped against what I took to be a window sill, and started to sketch the entrance. Immediately I knew I was being watched from behind. I didn't turn round, carried on drawing, and let what would happen happen. How I knew what I saw/felt I don't know, but I know that the mother of the house had been preparing some food, and came to the 'window' to see who was there. She had with her her little girl who asked her mother what I was doing. The mother then picked her up, so she could see. I dared not turn round for fear of losing 'contact'. On completion, I called my boyfriend, who was ready to leave. He felt nothing, or saw nothing. But again as we left the village I had the pleasant feeling of saying goodbye to a friendly community."

Carn Euny fogou

---

[68] Jackie Sutton *A Close Encounter at Carn Euny* [Meyn Mamvro, no.21 p.15]

Many other people have also reported feeling of great peace and tranquility at Carn Euny, but this appears to be a genuine 'time slip' experience brought about through sketching, a creative activity that led to an altered state of consciousness. It is worth remembering of course, that Carn Euny fogou was one of the sites chosen for the Dragon Project Dreaming Sessions [see Ch.10].

Another fogou site, where many experiences have been recorded is Boleigh [SW4370 2520], where, until recently, there was a Centre for Alternative Education and Research (CAER) run by a psychotherapist Jo May. Jo's book *Fogou: a journey into the Underworld*[69] tells the story of how he came to feel that he was the 'guardian' for the site, and some of the psychic connections he made at and with the site:
"The only sounds (in the fogou) are your breathing and heartbeat. And then the voices come. You want to cling to reality and block the voices out. But they are insistent, and you listen because although you hear them with your mind, they speak with a voice that is not your own. And locked in here for centuries, they want to be heard."

These voices spoke to Jo of some of the ancestors who lived at the courtyard house settlement there, and he began to have visions of them and see their faces and hear them speak. A figure of a woman in white was seen by visitors to the place and Jo had an OOBE and a visit from "the old ones". He says: "There were so many synchronisities, psychic messages and even psychic phenomena". He also believes that the settlement there was the "sacral centre (of the area), the seat of the will, the energy vibrating here at a lower rate, manifesting itself as devas and nature spirits and other energetic forms" and that what emerges in the fogou is a pattern involving synchronous imagery, inner voices and visions, and energy effects experienced at a bodily level. "It seems clear that the fogou was used as a focal point for spiritual practices involving death and rebirth, vision quests, healing, inner guidance and soul-making".

In an article in *Meyn Mamvro*[70] Jo said: "The kind of phenonema experienced in the fogou – on several occasions by a number of people simultaneously – include inner voices giving uncannily pertinent guidance, sometimes forecasting events before they happen; subjective perceptions of powers and presences – usually of female figures, frequently described as

---

[69] Jo May *Fogou* [Gothic Image, 1996]
[70] Jo May *Living with a Fogou* [Meyn Mamvro, no.3 p.7-10]

78

'woman in white'[71] or priestesses; visions involving fire, symbolic perhaps, of inner cleansing; visions involving the laying out of the dead – usually bedecked with flowers – in preparation for the soul's journey to another realm; visions of enforced entombment for the purpose of confronting the dark side of the soul in order to re-emerge reborn; experiences of people being 'called to the fogou to symbolically 'die' or else to collectively grieve someone who actually has died; experiences of waves of peace or comfort, and stilling of inner turmoil".

Boleigh fogou – entrance to the Underworld

The fogou has had a dramatic effect on some people. One person I know simply cannot go down there: she finds the power there too overwhelming while another just wants to curl up and sleep down there. Sometimes the fogou itself can seem not to want you to enter: someone else had a strange experience the first time she went to Boleigh. When she got there she found the entrance was covered over by two large megalithic slabs, completely blocking the way in. Thinking this was normal, she returned, only to be told later by someone that of course there was no barrier to the entrance. When she went back again, there were no entrance stones, but she swears to this day that they were there when she first saw it, and were much too huge for anyone to have casually put there and taken away later.

---

[71] A 'woman in white' figure has also been seen at the entrance of Pendeen fogou [SW3837 3553]. She appears on Christmas morning, with a red rose in her mouth and is said to portend death to anyone who sees her. She may be a folk memory of a Goddess.

Sometimes, the energy or power in the fogou seems active or even malignant (or is it simply the way individual people respond to it?). One person had a ring she was wearing literally wrenched off her hand while she was down there in a way she has never been able to explain. Others have always found the atmosphere very peaceful, almost soporific. The following account is by a woman, K.G, who knows the fogou well:[72] "The fogou has become a gateway to the underworld for me; it helps me reach within myself levels of dream and vision which enrich and add meaning to my life and my pictures (I am an artist). That is not to say that the transition is always easy. The fogou has at times had odd physical effects on me, cramping stomach pains. Once I was overtaken by acute dizziness, often it seems dark and unwelcoming. It is different on different occasions, or perhaps it is I who am different and at times not ready to experience its depth on my own. Going into a fogou, I meet myself".

KG goes on to recount a vision she had in the fogou of a wedding, which she felt was of relevance to her life at the time, symbolizing an inner process of male-female harmonization and confirming that it was all right for her to re-marry. Another woman who had a dramatic experience in the fogou was Geraldine Andrew:[73] "We stood quietly while four small candles pricked the darkness and gave solace. We allowed the energy from our bodies to flow down into Mother Earth. I was feeling content and peaceful, breathing deeply as I felt the deep connection with the earth. Then, the only way to describe the next sensation was as 'a bolt from the blue'. The force was immense: it was a spiralling force in the centre of my forehead, the spin was so strong, and quickly became faster and faster. I felt sick, my whole body reeling. I felt my head would explode. I could no longer stand, my knees were collapsing and I fell to the ground. As I fell, the energy left me as suddenly as it had appeared. I was very shaken and was helped back to the kitchen".

The significance of this 'energy shot' in the fogou for Geraldine seems to have been a dramatic turning point in her life, as she says that from that time her life changed, an acceleration of energy and consciousness. She says: "I believe these sites focus the potential of the human, spiritual mind, and by concentrating and understanding the nature of this force we can raise ourselves to the status of the God/Goddess within ourselves".

---

[72] K.G *Spirit of the Fogou* [Meyn Mamvro, no.9 p.16]
[73] Geraldine Andrew *Dor Dama* [Meyn Mamvro, no.18 p.20-1]

Finally, there is a fascinating account of some 'time slip' experiences by Pamela Cox[74], who seems to have particularly well-enhanced visionary powers (perhaps the fact that she is partially sighted allows these to manifest). In 1992 she and her husband and daughter visited the Nine Maidens Stone Row near St.Columb [SW9363 6745], the site of the CEMG dowsing day [see Ch.2]. She 'saw' a variety of things that are not now there, including a small ring of stones about 12ft in diameter, and a line of stones leading to another small circle surrounding the westerly stone of the row. Previously (in 1989) both she and her husband had 'seen' a double row on stones on Crantock Beach near Newquay that are no longer there, and the surrounding countryside had looked completely different from how it is today. In 1965 they had visited the Cheesewring on Bodmin Moor and seen a long double avenue of stones leading towards the rock formation on the western side. No such row has ever been recorded, but, interestingly this is a place that archaeologist John Barnatt has suggested would have had a processional way leading from the Hurlers stone circle [SX2584 7146] to the Cheesewring [see Ch.2].

A similar kind of vision was experienced by a woman (DE) in West Penwith near to Tregeseal Circle [SW3866 3238]. In a shift of reality experience, she saw a winding stone row leading from the circle to Carn Kenidjack about half a mile away. She also seems to have had some kind of time slip experience, because she also saw a line of people in cloaks walking along the row in a slow ritualistic kind of way. The same thing happened to Geraldine Charles who saw "with a kind of double sight" three circles at Treen Common stone circle/enclosure [SW4446 3666] where now there is only one.

So what do all these experiences mean? Obviously, at particular times places and circumstances, certain people are able to have experiences of a psychic or visionary nature. Usually quite involuntarily, they enter an altered state of consciousness, during which time they might see or experience the site as it was, and/or be affected by the energy field at the site which interacts with their own emotional state. This might take the form of a vision, or be manifested in a dream, both of which seem as real as the waking everyday state. Often the 'seer' is changed by the experience, or their life takes a different turn after the experience. These places and these sites are like portals into a different reality, or a different time frame - truly an opening of the veil between the worlds.

---

[74] Terry Cox *Visions of stone rows* [Meyn Mamvro, no.21 p.16-17]

CONCLUSION

We have travelled a long way and covered a lot of ground in this book. From the notion of straight lines across the land (leys), we moved into anomalous energies (energy lines, radiation, magnetism, sound and light energies). From there, we looked at how the ancient sites were deliberately aligned to the sun, moon and stars, and then the last 4 chapters turned to the world of spirit: ghost roads, mythic pathways, fairy paths, journeys to the Otherworld, and altered states of consciousness. Along the way we have encountered many strange happenings, unexplained anomalies and paranormal experiences at or near ancient sites in Cornwall. It has been a veritable cornucopia of strangeness!

But now, at the end, can we draw any conclusions from this myriad of insights and experiences at the megalithic sites in Cornwall? I don't want to falsely suggest some kind of "unified theory" that explains it all, but I do think there are common links between all of these things. They can perhaps be best summarised as follows:-

Our prehistoric ancestors were probably much more in tune with the earth and its place in the cosmos than we are today, surrounded as we are by so much artificial electricity, light and other energies. They could probably sense or dowse minute changes in the patterns of power and energy that flow through this earth. They were aware of changes in the radiation, the electromagnetic fields, the light anomalies, and the strange sounds that sometimes can be found in certain rocks and stones, and manifest in particular places. At these places they built their monuments: the quoits, burial chambers, stone circles, standing stones, and later the fogous. These sites did not exist in isolation but were linked together throughout the land, by being placed in straight lines or significant patterns in the landscape, or were deliberately aligned to significant hills and tors, often so that the rising and setting sun and moon could be seen, observed and celebrated at significant time of the year. They would also go to these places in order to go on shamanic journeys to connect with the spirits of the dead or the ancestors, and this is remembered in old stories and legends of piskies, spirit paths and the Otherworld. At some of these places nowadays people continue to have visions and connections with that World, or with the strange energies manifested at these places.

I can do no better than to end with a quotation from Paul Devereux, who has done so much to awaken our curiosity about these phenomena, and to whom the whole field of "Earth Mysteries" owes a huge debt:

"We may discover that altered states at sites with special properties allow entry to highly specialised orders of consciousness which give direct access to the energy body of the Earth. It may be that alpha, theta and delta brain rhythm states, induced by physical contact at a specific time with a naturally magnetic stone implanted in the ground, or by a heightened radon atmosphere, could allow us to key directly into the great 10-15 cycle-a-second electromagnetic rhythms of the planet, and allow our consciousness to resonate at global levels"[75].

There is much that we have discovered about some of these states, and much that has been uncovered about anomalous happenings at some of these sites, but it is all only the tip of an iceberg. There is so much more to be found out and discovered, and it may well be that as the 21st century unfolds that much of which is still mysterious and 'paranormal' becomes more readily known and understood. As far as Cornwall goes, we are all only just beginning to understand some of the secrets of these magical and sacred places. If we continue to visit them 'in the right frame of mind' then who knows what will be revealed to us in the future? The journey is an exciting and thrilling one. Enjoy the ride!

Cheryl Straffon

If you have visited any ancient sites in Cornwall, and experienced any unusual phenomena or gained any significant insights into the possible meanings of the site, then I would like to hear from you. Please write to the address on the inside title page, or e-mail cheryl.straffon@meynmamvro.freeserve.co.uk.

---

[75] Paul Devereux *Earthmind* [Harper & Row, 1989]

INDEX